ADRENALINE:
The Key to Your Behavior

ADRENALINE:
The Key
to
Your Behavior

L.B. HOLLINGSWORTH, M.D.

CHILTON BOOK COMPANY
RADNOR, PENNSYLVANIA

Copyright © 1973 by L. B. Hollingsworth
First Edition   All Rights Reserved
Published in Radnor, Pa., by Chilton Book Company
and simultaneously in Ontario, Canada,
by Thomas Nelson & Sons, Ltd.
Designed by William E. Lickfield
Manufactured in the United States of America

Library of Congress Cataloging in Publication Data

Hollingsworth, Lyman Burgess, 1910-
    Adrenaline: the key to your behavior.

    1. Aggressiveness (Psychology)   2. Adrenaline.
I. Title. [DNLM: 1. Criminal psychology.
2. Epinephrine—Adverse effects. 3. Psychopharmacology.
WK 725 H741a 1973]
BF575.A3H58   152.5′2   73-5767
ISBN 0-8019-5838-5

Contents

ADRENALINE:
The Key
to
Your Behavior

1

The Enemy We Shelter

Man is the creature that
cannot emerge from himself...
MARCEL PROUST

THE bitter wind howling across the plains galvanized the squat figure into action. He pulled stones and pieces of timber in various sizes as near the door of the cave as he dared, piled them up, then knelt behind them out of the blast of chilling air to twirl a pointed stick in dried bits of kindling. When at last a thin wisp of smoke spiraled up, followed by a flicker of flame, he added wood until he had a sizable fire. The shaggy-haired woman and child with him helped by placing long branches in the edge of the flames so that the heavier ends would blaze up, leaving the far extremes outside the circle of intense heat. When the man judged the time to be right, he picked up one of the firebrands and flung it with a guttural yell into the depths of the cave. He followed it with another and still another, until the terrified beast inside dashed out in panic. The woman and child ran inside and quickly collected the burning torches into a pile in the center of the cave floor while outside the sounds of rage rose above the cry of the wind as the man attacked the animal with his crude weapon. When he later dragged the carcass into the cave, all three set to work barricading the entrance with stones and timber, while behind them the flames leaped high and cast wavering shadows on the dark walls of the cavern. When flesh had been torn from the animal with sharp rocks and heated in the coals, the three crouched around the burned-down fire and gorged themselves.

That scene or a similar one was undoubtedly repeated countless times in the early days of the human race. As many obvious differences as there were between family life then and our modern concept of it, there was one particular likeness. The head of that group had provided the basic life-giving needs—food, shelter and warmth. As he pitted his strength and cunning against that of the beast, adrenaline flowed into his system to give him added strength and endurance when he most needed it. After the battle was over, he felt a sense of satisfaction as he tore at the half-cooked meat with his teeth and felt the warmth of the fire seep into his body. The only indication of his pride in his achievement was probably in the satisfied grunt he gave before he rolled over and went to sleep with his back to the fire.

In one respect, that caveman of long ago was more fortunate than his modern counterpart. Although he lived with constant physical danger, his confrontation with it was quickly resolved. Either he killed beasts or the strange human beings who entered the area he regarded as his own or he was slain himself. His hostility flared up quickly and as quickly subsided or was extinguished by fang or spear. If he wanted a certain woman as a mate, he took her, or tried to. His feelings of anger or pleasure were as plain as printed signs. He had no reason to conceal inner turmoil, as human beings have found it increasingly necessary to do ever since. His life was simple. Modern life and stress are complex in the extreme.

To say that one way of life is good and the other evil is absurd, as ridiculous as saying that a tornado is more benevolent than an avalanche. Danger is danger, whatever form it takes. It is partly the length of time it takes to resolve the peril that makes the difference. There is a wide variance in effect upon those experiencing the fear which has a distinct bearing on their mental and physical well-being. If danger is quickly brought to a climax, the flow of adrenaline is there to provide the strength needed to meet the immediate demands of the body and to see it through the ordeal. Warriors, even severely wounded ones, have spoken of the "afterglow" of battle, the feeling of having done well against odds and of a sense of accomplishment.

But the great tide of evolution has carried the human race past many of the short-term benefits that the surge of adrenaline supplied in the days of prehistory and early history. The development of the race has for the most part replaced brief, dangerous encounters with complicated, drawn-out anxieties that cannot be decided by a skillful thrust of a spear or a lucky strike with a stone. Thus the flow of adrenaline that once served such a vital purpose is now called upon again and again in ever-prolonged situations until its effect upon the human body has become something quite different from what it was.

The caveman demonstrated prime unconditioned reflexes— hunger, sex, aggression and flight. He was not capable of sustained anger or involved planning. When danger presented itself, it was dealt with swiftly and decisively. If he happened to be the loser, that was accepted matter-of-factly by his companions. Grief, if it existed at all as we know it, was submerged in the beginnings of mystic and supernatural stirrings in the minds of the onlookers and had not approached the refinements of present-day human emotions.

Early man dealt with sudden danger and fear by logical action. His smaller brain in its heavy encasement of skull was geared to whatever reaction the moment demanded—the use of a weapon if he happened to be carrying one or a grab for a nearby stone or stick or, at worst, swift flight from the area of danger. It is doubtful that he ever indulged himself in the sport of torturing another human or beast for the pleasure of it. His drives were direct and speedily satisfied without the embellishments of cruelty lacking apparent reason. His motives were part and parcel of his unconditioned reflexes.

Civilization, a term usually mouthed with pride, has brought with it revelations of the complexity of man's behavior, some of it as dark as the far side of the moon. All the advances of the humanities have not been as inspiring as those who chronicle the progress of the species would like them to be.

Much undesirable human behavior can be traced to two tiny adrenal glands in each person's body, one gland above each kidney. They weigh scarcely one fourth of an ounce, but they have a greater blood flow for their size than any other organ of the body. Every minute, a volume of blood approximately six times their weight circulates through them, facilitating the rapid outlet of adrenaline into the general circulation. Each adrenal gland, though so small, is a double organ having a cortex, or outer part, and a medulla, or inner part. Each is composed of distinct types of tissue which have different functions.

Adrenaline itself is a hormone secreted by the adrenal medulla and carried throughout the body. Its purpose is to regulate the functions of certain tissues and the rates of many metabolic processes. The word "hormone" comes from a Greek word meaning to excite or to arouse, which is exactly what the secretion of the adrenal glands does. Nerve impulses play an important part in the neuroendocrine system; a structural linkage exists between nerves and endocrines. Their alliance is so intimate that secretions of the adrenal medulla serve functionally as an extension of the nervous system. This is a highly significant fact, since it indicates that psychic influences modify the activity of the adrenal medulla and the secretion of adrenaline from it.

The medulla is the soft, reddish, inner part of the adrenal gland and it secretes adrenaline after being stimulated by sympathetic nerves directly connected with the hypothalamus in the brain. The medulla's role is to activate emotional impulses in emergencies and therefore to help the body to adjust to adverse environmental conditions. Medical science has not been able to attribute any known disease to the hypofunction of the medulla; but a tumor of the medulla may be behind such dramatic disturbances as a sudden marked increase in blood pressure, violent heart action, tightness in the chest, a feeling of apprehension, a throbbing heart, a sensation of heat or an uncontrollable tremor.

The cortex, or outer part, of the adrenal gland produces its secretion after being stimulated by pituitary hormones. This adrenal steroid secretion contributes to the regulation of various mechanisms in the body—electrolyte balance, carbohydrate and protein conversion and use, resistance to shock and infection, protection against various types of stress, bodily growth and the development of the sexual functions. Perhaps the most important hormones produced by the adrenal cortex are those of the cortisone family. Synthetic hormones of this group—hydrocortisone, the "meti" cortins and others discovered only recently—have been used successfully against some one hundred diseases.

The adrenal cortex is essential to life. When the adrenal medullas are removed, their function is taken over by sympathetic nerves which secrete adrenaline and noradrenaline at nerve endings, by the hypertrophy (excessive growth) of adrenaline-producing "rests" (cells or displaced fetal tissue embedded in tissue of another character) and by the increased activity of ganglia, or nerve cell concentrations, lying outside the central nervous system.

Before 1942 the medulla was believed to secrete only adrenaline. Then a second hormone, called noradrenaline, was identified. Almost identical to adrenaline, except for a certain difference in its chemical composition, both it and adrenaline are found at sympathetic nerve endings, where the two secretions serve to transmit impulses between nerves and muscles. Both appear to be present in the hypothalamus in greater concentrations than in any other part of the brain.

There are groups of cells, called chromaffin cells, at various sites throughout the body which produce adrenaline. This substance can either constrict or dilate smaller blood vessels, causing high blood pressure by augmenting the force and rate of heartbeat and by increasing the cardiac output of blood. Noradrenaline, on the other hand, acts primarily as a vasoconstrictor. It produces high blood pressure by heightening resistance to the flow of blood near the skin, an activity in which it is from one to four times as active as adrenaline itself. However, it increases oxygen consumption and heartbeat much less than adrenaline does. It also increases blood sugar to a much lesser degree and if administered to a patient it does not affect the central nervous system with restlessness or emotional distress, as happens after an injection of adrenaline.

Adults who are chronically angry have considerable amounts of both adrenaline and noradrenaline in their bloodstream, although noradrenaline is the predominant factor in those whose anger is directly projected toward the outside world at large, while adrenaline is prevalent in those whose ferocious tendencies are vented inwardly, producing an accompanying anxiety. The former is characteristic of infancy and childhood, while the latter usually increases with physical maturity simply because human conditioning to fear has the effect of driving outward anger underground, as it were. In such cases, "growing up" merely disguises the symptoms and frequently intensifies them because of the veil of secrecy the individual feels compelled to draw about his emotions in order to conceal them. What often appears to be a process of maturing may actually be only a clever or even an involuntary method of camouflage.

Behavioral scientists are searching for answers to the problems of juvenile delinquency, the irrational and dangerous actions of adults, sadism and many other "abnormal" forms of human conduct. Many scapegoats have been invented. Parents have of course taken the lion's share of abuse: they have been accused of being too permissive, too strict, too adoring, too aloof. Naturally, everything a person experiences from the moment of birth is recorded somewhere in the conscious or subconscious mind. Events or impressions which he does not even remember may well affect him in his later life.

It must be conceded that there are partial truths in almost every explanation offered for antisocial behavior. A burgeoning collective conscience seems to demand that the causes of all kinds of undesirable actions, from simple rudeness to criminal conduct, be ferreted out and dealt with. An army is at work trying scientifically to understand the human psyche, yet many diligent searchers miss the answers to much human misery because they lie so close at hand that they go undetected.

In many cases, the culprits are the tiny adrenal glands on the kidneys. They evolved so that the species could survive in its desperate struggle for existence. The course of human social development has thwarted nature's original intent, ironically made it damaging to the self: the secretions of these small glands have turned upon their host and threatened to destroy rather than preserve it.

2

Addicts Unaware

Things are in the saddle,
And ride mankind.
RALPH WALDO EMERSON

THE Stone Age lasted almost a million years. During that time, man learned to walk erect and to outwit the beasts of prey who stalked him. He eventually fashioned crude tools and formed the concepts of home and family. He hunted animals for food and clothing for himself and for those few other humans in close enough proximity not to be regarded as enemies. He felt the first, faint yearnings to fathom the mysteries of life and to form primitive, mystic alliances with forces he did not understand in order to protect himself from them. This activity, in turn, led him to develop his artistic capabilities. Cave paintings in many parts of the world attest to his considerable prowess in that endeavor. Still later, he found it unnecessary to live a nomadic life. He learned to plant and harvest and preserve food. Mud huts or other sturdy but temporary shelters were built in groups, giving him his first experience with the pleasures and perils of community life.

Eventually, refinements in various cultures evolved, differing because of geography, climate and available resources. The Stone Age gave way to a period loosely termed "historic times." Cities replaced some of the early settlements. Social structures were needed to provide rules and guidelines for a new way of life. Self-perception grew until human beings realized that they alone among all the creatures of the earth had a spiritual quality and a unique power to guide their own destinies to a certain extent. A number of religions gained followers and then believers to help assure them that they had not been cast upon the earth with as little purpose as pebbles thrown upon a shore by storm-tossed waves. They found ways to pass on to their descendants the experience they had accumulated. Temples and monuments were built that still stand. Ships plied the seas and fostered long-range communication among the peoples of the earth, mixing cultures and races.

At first glance, all of the advances seem to have been positive values. But the unrecognized problems of adrenaline remained to be dealt with. The violent man-to-man or man-to-beast conflicts which had characterized primitive times, when life or death depended on the full mobilization of all bodily reserves, were disappearing as a daily way of life. Less and less often were people called upon to save themselves through sudden bursts of strength and energy, activated by adrenaline.

Those who made the rules and set the values for their societies looked askance at overt acts of violence between individuals. Wars still raged at intervals, of course, but in their intervals the cause of peace was carried forward like a bright banner, at least verbally. Yet all the ideals and utopian visions did not stop the secretions of the adrenal glands. Since society frowned on open aggression and anger except under certain conditions, though, the feelings set in motion by this mysterious bodily function had to be concealed. The seemingly innate need for violence and conflict was subdued.

It was a slow process, ignored and unnoticed by the mainstream of human life. Conflict continued to seek and to find acceptable outlets whenever possible. Medieval knights still rode forth looking only for a stranger to fight. He did not have to be an enemy, merely another armed man. The "damsel in distress" was more often a handy excuse than a reality. Castles and fortresses came under seige simply as military exercises as readily as if a true dispute had existed. As long as the reason remained socially acceptable, aggression continued.

With the exception of outright war, the bounds of society's approval of aggressive behavior became narrower and narrower. The wealthier classes placed great emphasis on manners and social graces, and the lower social levels sought to imitate them. The so-called manners may have been largely artificial, but they were the style and therefore important.

Modern man will never know what atrocities were committed in the name of the Crusades, which had little or nothing to do with religion. Many Crusaders knew a good outlet when they saw one and exploited each opportunity as fully as possible. Adventurers and criminals made up much of the bulk of the bands, along with military men and merchants looking for new markets for their goods. The fact that the popes sanctioned them lent dignity to the assaults, and the cross that was the symbol for the various attacks made them seem holy in the eyes of the multitudes. There were even Children's Crusades in the thirteenth century which resulted in wholesale death for many youngsters.

A paradox existed for countless years and only a handful of the deepest thinkers realized its existence. The veneer of civilization was spreading, and keeping pace with it was an almost desperate need for violence. Even those brilliant minds who pondered the paradox knew next to nothing about the human neuroendocrine system and what the repression of primitive, animal-like behavior was doing to it.

The same vicious urges that prompted the Roman populace to watch lions attack Christians can be seen throughout more recent history. The American Indians periodically went on the warpath and slaughtered the first group of white men they met. The invaders from across the sea did the same thing to the red men. They did not usually seek out certain groups to attack. It was enough that they were strangers.

One specific incident in American history took place when John Colter and a companion were seized by Indians in the Territory of Montana in 1808. Colter allowed himself to be stripped of all his clothing while his companion, who resisted, was hacked to pieces. By sign language, the chief of the tribe ordered Colter to run across the prairie. When he had gone a little way, he looked back to see the young warriors putting everything aside but their weapons and preparing to chase him. Knowing his scalp would be the victor's prize, he ran away from the whooping pursuers as rapidly as possible. He told a contemporary later that his legs seemed to gather supernatural speed. He ran for approximately three miles before his strength began to wane. He slowed his flight, gasping for breath, and looked back to see only one of the Indians close behind him. The warrior tried to cast his spear at Colter but tripped and fell headlong. Colter wheeled, grabbed the spear and killed his enemy. He said then that his strength seemed to flow suddenly back into his body and he ran on to safety, feeling refreshed and fit.

Of course, what happened was a dual flood of adrenaline through his system at the two most critical points of his flight. This account is a prime example of a powerful negative drive, fearful flight, being converted instantly into a positive drive, the victorious kill. Colter's body's mode of preparation for both acts was the same. It was only his reaction which was altered to allow him to survive.

Many early explorers and mountain men have received adulation for performing similar feats. To say they do not deserve it would be unrealistic. But one aspect of such personalities should be given serious thought. It is possible that the men who lived on the rugged American frontiers chose that kind of life because their craving for excitement increased until nothing less than primitive danger satisfied them. Even the rough life in the new towns of the West was too dull for them. They may have had such an overpowering hunger for conflict and violence that they found it necessary to spend most of their time in areas where danger was so imminent that survival was a day-to-day struggle.

For a person who has such a need for physical danger, the next best thing to being a participant is being a spectator. This vicarious satisfaction is what brings out crowds at a prizefight to watch two men fight it out until one is beaten, stunned and bleeding. It is what fills the bullrings to overflowing in Spain and Mexico. It is what lined the streets of our own country with citizens watching in a patriotic frenzy while their own sons, brothers, husbands and fathers marched off to distant lands. It is the same puzzling fervor which makes a crowd watch a potential suicide tremble on a ledge high above them and even urge him to jump. Not many years ago a public hanging was an event not to be missed by stalwart men and some of their female counterparts. People still watch aerial acrobatics and death-dealing motor races with what must be pleasurable sensations—why else would they be so enthralled?

Just as eating a confection must be more enjoyable to some people than merely looking at it, they must find it more stimulating to engage in real conflict. A variety of emotions, plain cowardice for one, may lead them to choose the role of spectator. Either way, it cannot be denied that the need for stimulation is a strong impulse.

Frequent cries are made against the violence on television; yet many of the shows that enjoy perennial popularity sustain a high level of that commodity. Readers are often considered the mildest of people, but editors constantly urge writers to provide the one priceless ingredient—conflict—to assure sales for their novels.

What is the cause of this strange human fascination with danger? It is not an aberration because it occurs in many people who are mentally sound and physically normal. The stimulating effects of violence watched or experienced are similar to those obtained through the use of drugs. Many persons who fall within the bounds of what is normal would be outraged at the comparison, but the likenesses become more apparent under close examination. Thus we begin to understand the mystery of adrenaline.

Watch young children at play. Most of them act out real life situations in exaggerated forms. They spank dolls and strike one another. They mimic adult dissension. They ask for and receive as gifts toy guns and models of war-making mechanisms. They play "cowboy and Indian." Most of them are conditioned to practice conflict from an early age. If a child is kept from play which involves conflict, he is apt to engage in flights of fancy, and the world of fantasy can be more crowded with conflict than his real world.

Many children, by the time they reach their teens, are so conditioned for conflict that they are actually dependent upon it in varying degrees. They easily become restless and bored unless something exciting is taking place around them. It is difficult to determine what is to blame for this phenomenon unless one wishes to heap it on the nebulous catchall called "civilization"—a state the human race may not yet have remotely approached, considered in the light of possible future accomplishments.

What physical changes take place when danger threatens? The cortex of the brain perceives and evaluates the stimulus, then responds. The hypothalamus sends out somatic nerve impulses and sympathetic nerve impulses to alert the body to a state of alarm. Adrenaline is immediately released and it circulates rapidly. Activity in the digestive tract ceases. The mouth becomes dry as the saliva thickens. The depth of breathing increases, expanding the lungs and improving the flow of air. Cold sweat is produced by the sweat glands. Blood vessels near the surface of the skin become constricted, causing paleness. Abdominal blood vessels also undergo constriction, while those of the heart and large skeletal muscles expand. The heartbeat increases in rate and force. Blood pressure rises, sending blood gushing into the brain, heart, lungs and skeletal muscles. Muscular fatigue is relieved by the adrenaline in the bloodstream, and strength and stamina are increased. The spleen automatically contributes to the process by emptying its reservoir of red cells into the bloodstream. Together with an accelerated circulation and an increased exchange of air in the lungs, that augments the distribution of oxygen and the removal of waste materials throughout the body. The liver and the muscles also deliver stored sugar to the circulation in order to provide immediate fuel for flight or battle. The liver sends out substances which shorten the clotting time of blood so that every possible drop will be available in case of bodily injury.

The ancients spoke of what they termed the "tripod of life," meaning the heart, the lungs and the brain. Those organs, together with the skeletal muscles, are the recipients of blood taken from less important parts of the body at times of stress or threat. As all of these physical changes take place, the stimulation of the central nervous system sends adrenaline out as a reserve force in the battle for life. Since adrenaline has the power to block certain nerve junctions, it can limit the transmission of nerve impulses that are not directly concerned with survival. This enables the mind to ignore many ordinary stimuli and to concentrate on the emergency at hand. Cortical centers, the seat of peripheral pain, are numbed; hence, a person may be injured and not distracted by pain. Indeed, he may not even realize he has been hurt. His mental processes are vitalized and energized. He experiences a sense of well-being and mental intoxication with an ensuing surge of power. Feelings of superiority and increased courage are whirlwinds which sweep aside the boredom and monotony of everyday living. Joy in being alive is strong. At this moment, the person reaches one of life's highest peaks.

There is a strange alliance at work at such a time. The mere injection of adrenaline into the body produces the usual physical changes—the cessation of movements of the stomach and intestines, the constriction of mesenteric vessels and an increased heartbeat. Yet, without stimuli from the environment, the chemical effects of adrenaline are limited to visceral responses and have no effect on the emotions.

When all the forces combine, many people reach a state of pleasurable and emotional intoxication. They seek dangerous situations. They so enjoy strife that they come to love the fear which is its forerunner. Peril is not something to be escaped from. It is welcomed as a means to an end.

Since modern life is largely devoid of the daily tooth-and-nail struggle to sustain life, human beings who have been conditioned to need conflict and its resultant feelings of joy find themselves in the position of having to create their own strife. Most of them would be outraged at being compared with alcoholics or drug addicts, yet the fact remains that a similarity exists. Those who depend on liquor or drugs are small in number compared with the total population. They seem numerous because they are conspicuous by their behavior when they are under the influence of either artificial stimulant. Far less evident are those people who harbor a desperate hunger for adrenaline stimulation in situations of conflict. They look and act like anyone else. The difference is an insidious one. The hormone in their adrenal glands can be held back only so long by social disapproval. Then, without warning, it explodes in violence. Purely aggressive impulses, suddenly released, can be as devastating as acts brought on by drunken rages or as drug-influenced criminal deeds.

At the risk of oversimplifying the case at this early point in our discussion, it may be stated openly and directly that many of our social evils today can be traced directly to the very real addiction by many people to a hormone whose original purpose was to protect life. Because the threats against life today are just as terrifying, though more remote, such people have come to depend on adrenaline in combination with real or manufactured conflict to give them their thrills.

3

Forces that Combine

This sadness, this echo of pain;
A curious legend still haunts me,
Still haunts and obsesses my brain.
          HEINRICH HEINE

IT is important to repeat that the tiny adrenal glands to which such significance is attached do not activate themselves. The brain is the great decision-maker, although even its highly complex processes are influenced by conditioning from many sources. In less sophisticated times, the brain was widely considered to be something like a central switchboard in the body, there for the purpose of answering calls and sending messages to the proper places in the human organism. Now that computers have assumed such an important place in our lives, a more nearly accurate statement is that the brain is the body's computer. When one looks at the size of a manmade computer, it is all but impossible to believe that the brain, which on the average weighs slightly more than three pounds, could control so many vital bodily activities. What makes the small size of the human brain stranger still is that it contains expendable areas. One of the four main parts, the cerebrum, has sections which can be removed without dulling or changing mental ability. Tumors have been found which required the removal of all or part of the frontal lobe, yet its removal had no effect on the patient's normal functions. Thus, in some instances, this amazing organ does not even need all of the small space allotted to it.

The brain handles with dispatch all stimuli to the body. It is a miracle most people take for granted. This delicate mass is encased in the skull and suspended in cerebrospinal fluid for protection, because once brain cells are destroyed they cannot replace themselves as certain cells in other parts of the body do.

In addition to its generally known role, the brain serves as a storehouse for impressions. It has been proven that the intricate storage methods actually strengthen old memories in direct relation to the time they have been stored. Amnesia victims furnish the bulk of this proof. After a severe blow on the head, a person may become aware of reality with the firm conviction that time is in the past. He may have no memory whatsoever of recent events. As recovery occurs, memories return but always in the same order—from the past to the present. People of advanced age or mentally ill persons who have had shock treatments also demonstrate this old-memory theory. They remember events of long ago vividly while recent ones are hazy or missing.

The reception and storage capacities of the brain are difficult to comprehend. Some areas of brain research are comparable to uncharted seas, even to the medical scientist. For instance, a diversity of opinion exists concerning the extent to which the hypothalamus, which lies deep within the brain, and other components interact to control emotional behavior. They are, of course, all interconnected, but their individual roles in emotional responses are incredibly complex. In fact, the hypothalamus is a most frustrating area to explore. Naturally, a human hypothalamus in a living body can be examined only under the most restricted conditions of necessary surgery. The hypothalamus of the rat is the next best experimental arena, but it is only the size of a pin's head. In it lie numerous nuclei and fiber tracts. Attempts to learn more about them are further complicated by the fact that some of the tracts, which have no relation to the hypothalamic nuclei in a direct capacity, extend through, in and around the hypothalamus. Thus it seems impossible to be certain that experiments prove the theories for which they were devised.

In this century, several scientists have performed experiments on cats. They found that what seemed to be full-fledged rage could be achieved by electrically stimulating some areas of a cat's hypothalamus. In other experiments, all of the neural tissue above the hypothalamus was taken out. After stimulation, the rage pattern persisted. Some scientists called this "sham rage" or "pseudo rage." Scientists disagreed over whether it was only an outward show of rage or real rage. Different levels of anger were noted in various experiments, possibly because at least one of the scientists did not set down the exact location of the electrodes' placement in the hypothalamus. That could have been why reactions varied. At times, fear and flight resulted instead of attack.

The above is mentioned merely to illustrate the complexity of human emotional behavior. Even in lower animals, research is difficult to substantiate. It is clearly understood that the hypothalamus controls behavior through two separate mechanisms. It controls the activity of neurons in the brain stem and also exerts major control over the endocrine glands. It is capable of directly releasing hormones. In spite of the staggering amount of research which has been done, the mysteries of the human brain will remain as much a frontier as outer space for a long time to come.

There are connections between nerve cells called "synapses." Impulses can cross these spaces in one direction only. Extremely high magnification is needed before these spaces can be distinguished in the laboratory. There are different kinds of snyapses, but they all have to do with transmission. Thousands of them can be found in parallel arrangement. So as not to become too technical, suffice it to say that synaptic impulses are important in transmitting signals to various parts of the body. Their role in conditioning underlies a major premise of this book.

Conditioning as a powerful force was first brought into prominent public notice by Ivan Petrovich Pavlov, who taught at St. Petersburg's Medical Academy. Although most of his experiments took place half a century ago, they are still valuable to modern psychology. He is best known among laymen for his experiments with dogs and their salivary glands. Everyone who gave it any thought realized that when food was given to a dog saliva flowed generously from his glands. Obviously, the odor of food could produce the same reaction. If a dog had been accustomed to a certain food, the sight of it could cause his salivary glands to react. But a puppy that did not recognize the appearance of a certain food did not react in that way if he could not smell the food. Since the puppy had to know that the particular food could be enjoyed before he reacted in the usual manner, it proved that the action of the salivary glands was a "learned" or "conditioned" response.

Pavlov went on with his conditioning experiments, progressing from giving a dog food at the same time a buzzer sounded to pressing the buzzer in the absence of food and gaining the identical salivary response. Thus the sound became a conditioned stimulus, just as food alone was an unconditioned stimulus. Pavlov continued until he got the same action from the salivary gland by touching a certain spot on the animal or by showing him a light. He even used increasingly painful electric shocks and punctured the skin. As long as he saw to it that the dogs associated this process with the quick arrival of good food, they did not show any signs of displeasure. Their mouths watered and they reacted as they would in a thoroughly pleasant situation. Pavlov demonstrated the power of conditioning. Even pain could be overcome.

A possible relation to hypnotism can be seen here by the perceptive reader. Careful conditioning can produce almost any sought-after result. Further experimentation involving people indicates that, once a conditioned reflex is "set," it becomes involuntary. It happens without conscious effort.

The repetition of certain sequences will lead to automatic responses requiring neither effort nor above-average intelligence. Worms obviously rank low on the intelligence scale. Yet it is possible for a worm to adopt one course of action over another, based on reward and punishment. One clever experiment consisted of placing a worm in a T-shaped enclosure. It crawled from the bottom toward the top, since there was no other direction to go. If it turned to the left at the top, it got an electric shock. If it turned toward the right, it found a cozy bed of mud to crawl into. It took many trials to get the message to the worm, but it could be accomplished. The startling fact is this: if the worm is cut in two, the front end will grow a new tail and the tail will grow a new front end, resulting in two complete worms. If they are then put through the same process, both worms will invariably turn toward the mud! The memory of previous experience is stored in both halves of the worm and is somehow transmitted to the new half.

Conditioning, when applied to children by parents, is more often inadvertent than deliberate. Thus fear-conditioned parents are likely to raise fear-conditioned children unless the children are unusually strong-willed and can throw off fearful feelings when they are old enough to understand them. Conditioning is such a powerful force that it sets the pattern for complete lives. It is responsible for countless social ills and attitudes.

The various kinds of conditioning are so much a part of adrenaline dependence and its inherent dangers that few people really understand the relationship. Just as the caveman reacted directly and unhesitatingly to any stimulus, one segment of our society does the same, the very young. Most of the rest of us are too inhibited to respond honestly in most situations. Many of us are enmeshed in an elaborate game of covering up our impulses, and it is more detrimental to our health and well-being than you would imagine.

4

Childhood–The Molding of the Clay

As yet a child, nor yet a fool ...
ALEXANDER POPE

DURING the first forty-eight hours of a child's life, loud noises and loss of support are the natural, unconditioned, danger stimuli for the reaction of fear. A limitation or hampering of bodily movement is a stimulus for anger. In very early life, an infant can be shown a white rat at close range. He will not exhibit any sign of fear. However, if a loud noise is made at the time the rat is held close to the child, he will show fear. If it happens on several occasions, the sight of the rat without the accompanying sound will arouse visible fear. The rat has become a *signal* of danger, and the infant has undergone his first conditioning.

Infants come into the world quite equally equipped. Of course, mental capacities vary from low subnormal to brilliant, with most mentalities falling in the middle of the spectrum of intelligence. Mental capacity is largely established at birth. Its expansion comes later through education. Talent is innate—it can be developed or it can lie fallow. Emotional sensitivity is more highly developed in some infants at birth than in others, but sensitiveness is largely acquired or conditioned. The emotional traits of a small child can be likened to artist's clay. By the training they bestow upon a child, parents can shape the little life into one kind of individual or another.

Because exposure to modern social influences which condition one to react fearfully tends to blunt or curb aggressive tendencies, there are few entirely extroverted, aggressive individuals today. In terms of the pure conflict patterns of the

21

Stone Age, a wholly extroverted aggressor could hardly exist today. In our culture it is a rare individual who overtly murders a close relative because he grows old and begins to complain unceasingly. It would be all but impossible to find a person who would willingly go into a jungle prepared to attack a ferocious beast with only a sharpened stick or a crude stone implement. So the personality types we choose to call extroverted or aggressive are only relatively so.

On the other hand, purely introverted nonaggressors are everywhere, for we live in an almost totally fear-conditioned culture. The introverted, nonaggressive type of child is one who displays a negative and withdrawn attitude toward life in the realms of thought, emotion and action. Like other children, he starts out in life outwardly aggressive as nature intended. But somewhere along life's way the unpleasant emotional reaction of fear becomes so instilled in his personality that his permanent behavior pattern is predominantly fear conditioned and dominated by a negative drive.

In this state the primitive fighting urge of the child's personality may be almost completely repressed by fear-conditioning. A youngster so conditioned is afflicted with a grossly distressing nervous anxiety. Sometimes the burden of unpleasant anxiety is alleviated through the release of the drive by way of sublimation or through externally expressed hate. Such hate, added to the personality of a fear-conditioned individual, can potentiate a juvenile delinquent.

An introverted, nonaggressive child does not develop into an extroverted aggressor because he is continually exposed to unfavorable environmental influences which can produce only fear-conditioning. This often arises out of a frustrating family situation. The child fails to develop the necessary confidence and faith in the kindness and understanding of his parents and relatives. He does not learn how to make friends with other children. The people with whom he is in daily contact may have an unhealthy, introverted attitude toward life and may themselves be overly fear conditioned. In the home and in the surrounding environment, the child has few opportunities to express his positive drive through outward action. He is constantly curbed by parents and confining conditions. He experiences too little healthy emotional stimulation. He rarely feels a thrill of accomplishment in whatever he does, and the experience of emotional power is unknown to him.

Caught in the entanglement of modern social restrictions, the fear-conditioned child is rarely able to escape by physically running away. Therefore he may retreat to the only avenue of escape open to him—the recesses of his mind. Although the flight is purely imaginary, it has the same escape significance as an actual flight. But instead of the joy of release, he knows he has been defeated. His spirit is humbled. If he takes the beckoning path of mental retreat each time a dangerous situation threatens, he acquires an overabundance of muscular tension and nervous anxiety. He lives in a never ending state of nervous apprehension in which he continually anticipates renewal of the attack from which he has never been able to escape physically.

The usual result of such an escape mechanism is that the child develops an overly active imagination and begins to prefer to live in his imaginary world. He enjoys vicariously the action which fight-conditioned, extroverted individuals live realistically. He slips deeper and deeper into the world of fantasy until he accepts it as reality. In extreme cases, he becomes psychotic. This is such a tragic state that only parents who have watched it happen to their child can comprehend the horror of it. All parents should learn enough about what causes it to extend sympathetic encouragement rather than discipline toward a fearful child.

Most children tumble about and make noise as a natural part of their development. If a child in this normal pursuit is constantly told "Do this" or "You musn't do that" he may become quiet and uncommunicative. Instead of physically romping around, he will sit motionless in order to avoid trouble and mentally act out the activities forbidden to him. He learns to expect scolding and punishment whenever he shows excitement or causes the slightest disturbance. He is led to believe that anything that is fun is bad. Such impressions put him in poor emotional condition to meet the conflicts of the adult world later on.

Fear-conditioning in children is almost always the fault of the parents. Much of the time it is unintentional but just as harmful as if it were done maliciously. Parents who have unhealthy attitudes toward life spread their own fear-conditioning just as they would a contagious disease. A child is quick to sense anxiety, even though it remains unexpressed. Then, too, many adults incessantly complain about their misfortunes, comparing their possessions and opportunities with those of their neighbors, relatives or friends. While they are busy giving voice to their envy, unhappiness and disappointments and berating themselves because of what they call their own "bad luck," they may sneer at those they envy. They may complain that neighbors dislike them and that former friends have lost interest in them and no longer appreciate them. A child is a mirror, reflecting such unhappiness.

A divorced mother or an alcoholic father can, by his or her own self-depreciation, cause a child to feel like a social outcast, bringing him to bitterly reject himself and his family background. He often carries this burden with him throughout his life. Detecting weaknesses in the family structure and imagining hate and danger all around him causes a fear-conditioned scar to develop on his impressionable young mind. Most real scars become less noticeable with time, but this kind rarely diminishes in adulthood. In fact, it often sets a pattern for a person's role as parent. Feeling that his own parents were failures and that they let him down infects his behavior as a parent; he tends to follow the same awful pathway.

The introverted, nonaggressive child rarely runs afoul of the law. He stays out of trouble because the combative half of his personality has been so repressed by fear-conditioning that he practically never allows it expression in overt aggression against others. He even conceals his thoughts because he is afraid of being humiliated or laughed at if he tells what he is thinking or if he asks a serious question.

This type of child, if he is fortunate, may turn to philosophy or theology, seeking the real meaning of life and death and some satisfactory explanation for the horror of his childhood. It is surprising to contemplate, but the traits of retreating from reality are similar in highly respected scholars and in alcoholics, drug addicts and recluses.

A visual tip-off of a repressed child to anyone watching is the vacant stare he often has. He sits quietly with his thoughts, lost in dreams. He gazes into space, seeing nothing. If disturbed, he may be sulky and resentful. Such a child should be encouraged to make friends and to engage in the ordinary give-and-take of the world about him, conflict and all.

Among these introverted nonaggressors are the "bookworms," those who prefer to live vicariously through the pages of books. They become the heroes in books, suffering, fighting and conquering, barely tasting the emotions they should experience in full force. They are usually so quiet that parents hardly know they are there. A smug mother may say pridefully, "My boy has never caused me the least trouble." She may be absolutely correct, but she may have no idea of the violence going on in his mind beneath the deceptive quietude. Such a child may develop into a good or even an excellent student. He may give no hint of the resentment and hate he feels when he is ridiculed by others because "he always has his nose in a book." He may be driven to do his reading in secret, perhaps when he should be sleeping or studying something not to his liking, as if the act of reading were a sin.

Since a child of this type shrinks from rough play and the attacks of aggressive children, he usually stays at home to avoid the unpleasant conflict of the outside world. Other youngsters often call him a "square" or a "sissy." Parents sometimes resent his offishness. His father may be ashamed of his weakling and order, "Put up your fists and fight!" As a result, the child's hate may become twofold. He might hate his father for being a tyrant and himself for being "chicken." Such a child should not be taunted about his retiring attitude. Instead, he should be encouraged to participate in some sport he can learn to enjoy or even in which he might excel. He should be helped to understand that a certain amount of conflict and danger is necessary in life. He must learn that aggressive feelings are not "bad," indeed that they are vital in the right proportions. He must stand his ground and fight when circumstances warrant it. If he can run to his mom and be soothed by her tears when he gets a bloody nose, she is doing him a grave disservice. She won't always be there to run to when conflict overtakes him.

The first years of childhood are normally characterized by a relatively pure form of the primitive fight personality. But as the child grows older the dictates of modern civilization, and the retaliation of organized forces when the primitive fight personality reveals itself, lead to an inordinate calling up of fear responses. The resulting fear-conditioning then dominates behavior by repressing the primitive urge to fight.

When to discipline a child and at what age to discontinue it are questions that have been long and seriously debated. It is said that a whipping generation is followed by a nonwhipping generation and vice versa. Such is not always the case. Some children grow up to follow the patterns set by their parents. In such cases, both children and parents learn to associate noisy, exciting situations with punishment and cannot seem to shake off the conviction that the latter follows the former.

On the other hand, some parents who suffered indignities and cruelty as children vow never to inflict the same inhuman punishment on their children. So they lean over backward and refrain from punishing them when they truly need correction and guidance. Too little discipline can be as harmful as too much unless there is a great amount of shared love between parents and children. Youngsters who have had "soft" parents without the priceless ingredient of mutually understood love have an urge to fight which has never been satisfied. Thus they may grow up to beat their own children in order to fulfill this desire which they do not understand. It takes much discretion and freedom from dependence upon conflict and upon adrenaline stimulation to exert the proper amount of authority over a child. A young person who recognizes no authority at all is bound to become a problem.

When discipline is necessary, a parent should do his best to maintain a calm demeanor while administering it. It is helpful if he can wait until his own anger has cooled. There is nothing wrong with his saying, "When I get over being mad, I'll tend to you!" If a parent inflicts punishment of any kind when he is in a rage himself, his assurance that "this hurts me more than it does you" is rarely true, and the child knows it. If such a parent could be completely honest with himself, he would know that he actually enjoyed hurting his child. The excitement of punishing the child increased the adrenaline flow in his own body and furnished the stimulation he craved, the urge which drove him to the act in the first place.

A child who has deliberately misbehaved will be impressed with a sense of fairness if he realizes that he was punished after a cool and fair judgment, not because a parent got angry with him. The merits of kindly understanding and a gentle but firm voice cannot be overestimated. A child can detect emotional tension in the voice and mannerisms of an angry adult and can easily come to hate a person who punishes him in anger.

The "battered child" syndrome is more widespread than is usually recognized. The newspaper articles that tell of a father who, enraged by the continued crying of his own child, slapped or hit the infant so hard that it died give unknowing readers the impression that such a horrible thing seldom happens. Attacks upon helpless children are more frequent than the general public realizes. Some physicians are hesitant to report suspected cases of child beatings because parents may insist that the child fell or injured himself in some accidental fashion. The doctor is then at a distinct disadvantage. Usually he cannot prove that the injuries were inflicted willfully, and if he tries he may find himself involved in a lawsuit. He must be sure of his grounds before he makes an accusation.

Unpleasant as it is, the fact must be faced that there are

brutal parents. The threat to a youngster that if he does such and such a thing he will be "given the beating of his life" is not always just idle talk.

Verbal or physical punishment makes the home a place of torture for the little ones who have no power to strike back. And if one child among others in a family is singled out to be the victim of parental aggression, he may become so antagonistic that he develops into the "black sheep of the family." "Black sheep" are made, not born. It is well known that young people often commit acts which are far more devastating to themselves than to their parents in an effort to get even with them for inflicted abuses.

A child whose spirit has been broken by unreasonable hurt distrusts his parents and habitually reverts to the flight mechanism. In so doing, he becomes increasingly fear conditioned. He cannot deal with conflict and danger without undergoing an emotional crisis, without retreating in abject fear. Since physical retaliation is impossible because of his small stature, he can only retaliate on a mental and emotional level. He usually feels he has to be outwardly obedient and respectful, but there exists a burning, poorly concealed, resentful hostility which replaces the natural feelings of love and respect which he would otherwise have. This seething hatred produces a highly conditioned dependence upon adrenaline stimulation which urges him to seek conflict in order to gratify his own craving for mastery. It is a disastrously short step from hating a parent to hating society in general.

If a child tries to escape conflict and danger in his home by reverting to physical flight, he is often brought back to face further punishment. If the law discovers improper home conditions, the child may be removed to other surroundings, but that often comes too late to save him from his own ingrained tendencies.

Some of the most common home factors which can lead to hatred and aggressive resentment among children are:

A lack of mutual affection between parents and their children.

Overdominance by one or both parents.

Poor parental training to deal with life's problems as they come along.

A feeling of parental rejection arising from preferential attention paid one child over another.

A continual tendency in parents to blame and criticize without any compensating praise.

An open or hidden incompatibility of parents and voiced or implied threats of divorce.

Parents' economic failure.

Parents failure to develop in the child an attitude of give-and-take in a competitive world.

Cold, harsh, asocial parents.

A child needs constructive discipline above all else. Parents who exercise no control over a growing child or set no examples of gentlemanly and ladylike behavior fail to gain the respect of their young one. A child can love a parent who does not deserve that love, but respect must be earned. To gain respect, a parent must help a child learn to master his natural positive drives.

The fear of open conflict causes some children to make personal peace and safety their prime concerns. They shrink from worldly contact and are dismayed and frightened by any display of violence. Such a child will recoil from murder, violence, distress and other troubles portrayed on the screen, radio and television. The fact that in the playacting world the too aggressive individual is usually apprehended by the law further conditions him to know fear.

There are as many types of children as there are flowers or vegetables, but all of them require more careful nurturing than other growing things. Anthropologists have studied the culture of primitive peoples and have found important similarities and differences in their social culture and in ours. In some primitive tribes a child is taught from birth to distrust and fear members of his own and other tribes. In contrast, south sea islanders have traditionally reared their children to expect cooperation and kindness from others. Eskimos are quiet, mannerly people, and they pride themselves on the fact that they find it unnecessary to speak harshly to their children or to spank or beat them. Most Eskimo children are trusting and well behaved because they are taught not to fear or hate anyone. Some tribes in various parts of our world base their social and religious structures on brutality, murder and headhunting. Other tribes found their society upon the principles of kindness, trust and consideration. It is plain to see that all of these characteristics are the result of direct conditioning by family attitudes.

It seems an indisputable fact of life that if the members of a family seem calm and are gentle, any overly aggressive tendencies of a child are quieted and inhibited. On the other hand, if parents are jittery, tense, irritable and continually wrangling, the emotional effect of these overt conflicts is shared by the child. Arguments and quarrels can make a home a living hell for a youngster, and conflict in the home is most likely to condition the child to feel an inordinate urge to create exciting situations of danger, thereby laying the groundwork for the need for adrenaline stimulation.

One oddity in our culture is the "only child." People from larger family groups have a tendency to assume that such a child is always spoiled by too much attention. Admittedly, there are hazards to being a "one and only," but this is not one of them. Parental devotion to an only child makes him realize that he is an important part of a family who loves him. He does not suffer from the sense of parental rejection which in some other children produces feelings of fear and hatred, with the attendant high adrenaline stimulation. The real danger is that the parents of such a child may make the mistake of shielding him from the routine conflict of his childhood world. He may be overprotected, which will later prove to be a hindrance to his ability to cope with the challenging conflict of the adult world. He may be so flattered and pampered by the attention of his parents that when he gets out into the world on his own it will be difficult for him to adjust to the fact that he is but one of many competitors.

A contrasting situation is the one in which there are several children in a family. The firstborn's sense of self-importance is sometimes jolted by the arrival of a newcomer. He feels that he is being pushed out of his center spot. But the first one can be made to feel that the coming child is "his" as much as his parents'. In addition to the preparation, the first child should be allowed to hold and snuggle the new baby if he is big enough, thus strengthening the group acceptance of the little intruder. If this groundwork is not done well in advance, the first child may experience feelings of insecurity and danger, followed by fear. If remedial action is not taken, hatred and anger replace fear when the child's positive drive takes over as a survival response to regain the necessary sense of security. If the youngster is not soothed and comforted, his hatred and resentment increase and irreparable damage may be done to him.

All of that can be avoided if the child is made to feel important by sharing the responsibility for the new baby's safety and happiness. It is a good idea if he receives some small gift from his mother when she comes home from the hospital with the baby. Deep affection and loyalty between sisters and brothers is not inborn; it is learned. The saying "Blood is thicker that water" is nothing more than a few words strung together without the teaching process that must precede it. If great care is not taken to prevent jealousy of the new sister or brother, the firstborn may never recover psychologically.

Some unfortunate children suffer physical defects which cause them great suffering by making them easy prey for bullies. Other children, although fear conditioned themselves, know they can taunt afflicted children. This is the same primitive reaction found among animals in a jungle who fall upon and destroy a wounded member of their own group. Of course, children who have bodily defects should be afforded sympathy and help; more often, though, they are objects of poorly concealed contempt or bare hatred. Even parents are sometimes unable to conceal their dislike of such children. Such disfigured little mortals live a life of mental anguish along with an ever increasing fear-conditioning and a complete lack of self-confidence.

Some children with bodily defects spurn the proffered help of others because the offer itself only emphasizes the deficiency. Still other handicapped youngsters who are used to being petted and pampered at home grow up expecting to be favored because of their abnormality. A feeling of insufficiency causes both reactions. It is best all the way around if these children can be treated as if they were as near normal as possible. Allowances have to be made for the deficiencies, of course, but they should be glossed over as lightly as possible.

Danger and thrills are synonomous for many well-balanced children. Every adult can recall the feeling that the Ferris wheel seat at the fair was suddenly dropping out from under him. Yet he stepped out, flushed and exhilarated, at the end of the ride. The roller coaster was even better. The adrenal glands delivered a dizzying sensation of excitement to every part of the body.

At Coney Island recently, an eleven-year-old girl said the merry-go-round was too babyish, but she consented to go on an aerial ride with her father and then make the 250-foot parachute jump to the ground. As the two floated down, the parachute was snagged on a guide wire about halfway down. While horrified thousands watched from below, a park employee was lowered from above and freed the cable. When the little girl dropped into the safety net, she laughed and said, "It was fun!" This sensation of pleasure in the presence of peril is nature's way of giving people courage to face danger and to look forward to survival.

If there were not pleasure in danger, hot-rodders would not be driving on our highways hub to hub, playing their fantastic game of "chicken"—driving at high speed with steering wheels untouched, with the rule that the first one to grab the wheel to avert a crash is "chicken." Under questioning, these daring youngsters declare they were just having fun.

Critical dangers in rash adventure have an irresistible fascination. A challenge is produced which arouses fear, which in turn is thrilling. For many young people, the thrill of escapades far outweighs any worry of punishment that might follow.

A group of teenagers set out for home after picnicking on the nearly mile-wide Susquehanna River. Some of them took the trusty little steamer across the river. The rest elected to walk the ties of a railroad bridge. Halfway across, an engine suddenly loomed up. Some ran to the pier in back of them, some to the pier ahead, whichever was nearest. They all made it just in time. The experience made them "come alive," as they put it. Young people seem to so enjoy strife that they grow to love the fear which gives them strength for conflict. Danger is not just something to be escaped from; the fear it arouses is welcomed as an arsenal of augmented and glorious strength.

The first minutes and hours of infant behavior seem to be characterized by cries of wrath. Thus it appears that a child does not have to learn to be aggressive. He comes into the world already so equipped. Adding validity to this theory is the very slight sense of danger accompanying unrestrained aggressive thoughts and actions in unrepressed children under four years of age. That fact may be said to strengthen the general belief in the small degree of original fear in the human race.

There is a widespread but mistaken notion that little children are saddened by the sight of destruction and aggression. When children between the ages of one and two are put together in a playpen, they will pull each other's hair, bite one another, poke at eyes and grab toys without regard for ownership or the unhappiness that all of this causes in the underdog in the match.

At this stage of development, destruction and aggression play leading roles in their behavior. Young children at harmless play will puncture rubber balls, pull off the arms and legs of their dolls or soldiers, smash anything that is breakable and laugh happily about it. Admittedly, this may seem anything but "harmless" to the objects involved, but the minds of the children perceive no mischief in their acts. There is even a humorous aspect involved. When they have destroyed their toys to the extent that they can play with them no longer, they may cry as if they believed some hardhearted person was depriving them of the objects.

It has been well stated that there is a continual war raging in every nursery. It is at this time in an infant's life that aggressive and destructive impulses are at work which are very similar to those released in adulthood for the grim purposes of war. If two or more children are together in a nursery, it is necessary to watch them at all times so that they do not hurt each other.

Most adults are appalled at the idea of children seeing the rampant destruction of war. There is danger there, but it is not the kind the ordinary adult envisions. He is afraid that the child's delicate sensitivities may be upset by what he sees or that the child will be shocked into illness. On the contrary, the child will watch the destruction with primitive excitement instead of turning away in horror as expected. The real danger is that the aggression racing through the child will make him feel a oneness with the destruction raging in the world around him. He may absorb the feeling that this kind of destruction is acceptable in the world in which he lives. Children delightedly play around bomb craters and on bombed sites. They throw discarded bricks or broken objects they find at each other. In fact, under such circumstances it is next to impossible to get them to try to control their natural tendencies toward destruction. At this stage of their lives, they sould be learning to overcome and estrange themselves from the primitive, unacceptable urges of their infantile nature. If they are exposed to the horrors, atrocities and general beastliness of war, the experience nullifies the next natural stage of their development.

A child comes into the world with an inborn desire to be loved and protected, to be fed and kept warm. It is ironic that, within moments after his birth, forces set to work on him over which he has no control. He is fortunate if his parents are wise, for they will have more to do with his development than any other people on earth for the first crucial years. But later even they must yield to pressures beyond their complete control. By the time the child is old enough to go next door to play or to go to school, he will have to begin making his own decisions. They will of course be influenced by the people who have raised him until that time, but his own personality has by then been conditioned sufficiently to set him on his way to being an introvert or an extrovert, an aggressive or a nonaggressive person. Later forces can intervene, modify or even change him; but one thing is certain: many influences will be constantly at war to control his actions as long as he breathes.

To go full circle, back to the 48-hour-old infant mentioned at the beginning of the chapter, some most revealing experiments have been conducted concerning the close connection of the labyrinths of the inner ears and the adrenal glands, plus the important role that emotions play in combination with them. When a baby less than forty-eight hours old is dropped and caught in the air, the labyrinths within the ears are greatly disturbed by this sudden motion and strong nervous impulses are sent to alert the brain to danger. The brain in turn dispatches a message throughout the body and to the adrenal glands via the hypothalamus. Adrenaline is immediately secreted, an automatic reflex of fear is completed and the baby cries out. He may even vomit. Later, as the infant develops a tolerance to the stimulation from repeated falls, it laughs with pleasure. Such labyrinthine stimulation is an essential result of all fast motion.

In this way, the widespread use of the automobile has produced one of the first steps toward the mass conditioning of young people to high-level danger and adrenaline dependence by providing them with the thrills of speed. As we come to understand the fascination of faster and more dangerous motion, we learn to expect increasing numbers of hot-rodders. Speeding automobiles produce a situation of danger, sensed especially by the labyrinths of the ears (also sensed by the frightening sounds of accelerating motors and the blur of fast-moving landscapes). Danger produces fear. Large amounts of adrenaline are discharged into the bloodstream. They produce the thrills and stimulation which are the essence of all fast motion. Thus car manufacturers are practically forced to produce more powerful new models each year.

In considering the development of children, it becomes clear that they are unwitting products of conditioning. No all-accusing finger can be pointed at parents or teachers or any other group because, while some conditioning can be planned and controlled, some just happens. By becoming more aware of causes and effects, adults who want to work toward a better world can learn to exert more influence on constructive conditioning.

Before specific solutions can be advanced, some searching looks, however unsettling, should be taken at such deeply troubled members of our society as juvenile delinquents and criminals. They, too, are products of conditioning and adrenaline dependence. Many of them are victims of forces they cannot control. In order to learn to help them, we must thoroughly understand the problems that plague them.

5

Delinquency–Puzzle of Many Parts

Wealth is the parent of luxury and indolence,
And poverty of meanness and viciousness,
And both of discontent.

PLATO

How convenient it would be if delinquency could be pinned down to one level of society. We could place the blame on economic conditions or something else comparatively simple and begin doing something about it. But the most affluent communities produce delinquents, as do the most underprivileged neighborhoods. To further confuse the issue, many upright youths come from blighted areas. The reason for delinquency has been bounced around among a number of possible explanations, most of them proving to be oversimplifications upon close scrutiny. It is now generally accepted that various factors go into the making of a true delinquent. Adrenaline dependence is a major contributing force but this too must come about in conjunction with other influences. Just as we cannot claim that a war or a depression was brought on by any one event, we can only say that delinquency evolves from a combination of effects.

Before we approach the theory of adrenaline dependence, let us look at some of the other factors that play a part in the tragedy of delinquency. Poverty, deprivation and the stress of living in underprivileged neighborhoods prove to be too much of a strain for some personalities. Others seem to grow stronger as they struggle against their surroundings toward a worthwhile goal.

Many social workers assign parents most of the blame, referring to them as "delinquent parents." Many times parents are at fault, but the distinct fallacy in the reasoning of such social workers is that sometimes it is simply not applicable. A child may grow through adolescence into

37

adulthood, adoring and defending an errant parent. He constantly invents excuses for the parental weakness and never loses hope that the father or mother will eventually grow stronger. Often, he is determined to make up for all the "bad breaks" the parent has suffered. If for some reason the parent is committed to prison, that sometimes forges a link of loyalty that is stronger than ever. It is true, too, that a large percentage of juvenile delinquents come from shattered families, but they must be accorded only their proper share of blame.

Spoiled, overly pampered children are often pointed out as potential delinquents. This is unfair in the extreme. Such children may be too aggressive for the comfort of others. They may be obnoxious, but that does not make them delinquent. Children who have been severely disciplined may suffer from repressions which arouse their hatred and cause them to lean more toward delinquency. Yet even those children may have some good influence at work on them which keeps them headed in the right general direction.

Juvenile delinquency in certain respects is simply a reversion to the natural wildness or uninhibited behavior of the primitive ancestors of the human race. The saying "The kid went wild" is not far from the truth. Cattlemen state that cattle that stray into wild herds in remote areas often revert to the wild state. The same is true of horses. In our northern countries, well-trained Eskimo dogs turn wild when they run with undomesticated companions. It is said that even house cats, if loosed far from places of human habitation, quickly take on the characteristics of their wild counterparts. And the choicest rosebush soon grows out of bounds if it is not trimmed back.

Similarly, if a good boy gangs up with a group of bad boys, it is almost inevitable that he soon takes on the attributes of his lawless companions. He learns to swear, to steal things, to threaten people and to destroy property. When correctional officers release a boy from a reformatory, they invariably warn him not to consort with other delinquents. In most cases they are wasting their breath. By that time he is so conditioned to respond to the urge for excitement that he is likely to go out of his way to seek more and more of it.

Years ago, when rural life was more the natural order, circumstances did less to condition youngsters to pursue a life of rowdyism. Transportation and communication were not what they are today. Communities were more or less isolated. News was not promptly flashed to all parts of the country seconds after it became known. This fact alone kept bandits and killers from attaining widespread notoriety and the resultant youthful hero worship which tended to accompany their escapades. Life in small villages and on farms was quiet. The most exciting event of the week for the average boy was no doubt a trip to town on Saturday to buy the weekly supplies. Children received a minimum of exciting stimulation and had few opportunities to meet with and get to know evildoers. Children tended to remain more or less calm, simply because they had little choice. They might complain, rebel and finally leave home to find a new job and a fuller life, but they rarely indulged in unlawful excitement because they had never acquired a taste for it.

With the coming of widespread industrialization, most of that quiet living changed. There was a mass migration of rural dwellers to cities, where factories offered work at higher wages. Once urbanized, parents attained a higher standard of living while their children played and learned new things in a stimulating environment—the city. Many youngsters sought novel thrills and delighted in the change from the calm freshness of the country to the turbulence of the dirty city. The transplanted people often looked back at their old existence with nostalgia, but few of them actually went back to farm or village life. They chose to remain in the dynamic city because their craving for stimulating events and even for conflict had been so built up that they could not longer tolerate a quiet life in the country.

Then came the new, fast, exciting automobile. Driving a car gave young people a new feeling of power and independence. They could race out of sight of their parents and away from adult supervision. These were the most obvious thrills of the automobile. No one thought then of the less visible effects of speed on the human body, particularly young bodies. The facts described in the preceding chapter concerning the labyrinths of the inner ears and the resulting actions of the hypothalamus and the adrenal glands were unknown. But the newfound speed has excited the labyrinths of the inner ears of generations, causing the labyrinths to send out strong nerve impulses to alarm the brain to the threat of danger. The labyrinths control the sense of motion and equilibrium and are indirectly in communication with the hypothalamus in the brain. Nerve impulses from the brain excite the adrenal glands, which promptly release adrenaline into the bloodstream. Together, adrenaline stimulation and the fear aroused by speed have provided a new stimulation which is satisfied only by more speed. The need for more thrills on wheels causes some young people to become delinquents once they have exhausted the stimulation which the motor car has to offer.

The next step in seeking thrills may be to acts of vandalism. By then, the urge for excitement is out of hand, so these "addicts" look for kicks in burglary. Somewhere along the way they have learned the fascination of guns through television or comics, so they proceed to holdups with guns. If they are not caught or stopped, they may go to any length to gratify their craving for danger and adrenaline stimulation, as alcoholics will stop at nothing to satisfy the demands of their thirst. There is a marked resemblance in the compulsive pattern of behavior produced by dependence on adrenaline stimulation and that caused by drugs and alcohol—an exhilaration of the ego and a dulling of the sense of responsibility.

Divorce has already been mentioned as a contributing factor to some cases of delinquency, but even in families which stay together the fathers often suffer from an emotional breakdown caused by a general increase in fear-conditioning among men. Many modern men falter under the pressures of daily frustration and overstimulation which are followed by mental, physical and emotional reactions. The result is that some men become unwilling or unable to lend emotional support to their families.

This neutralizing of man's positive drive is a perilous social cancer which tends to make him a guest in his own household and a stranger to his children. During most of his waking hours, his family consists of a set of photographs in his wallet. He works for these photographed individuals, but he doesn't truly live with them. The mother usually tries to fill the breach by training her children to the best of her ability to become proper adults. But she cannot assume the role of both parents. Without the firm hand of a father to guide them, many children never acquire the controls which enable them to cope with their innate, normal but socially unacceptable impulses.

Various other factors involving family life may lead to delinquency. Parents are rarely, if ever, solely responsible for a child's delinquency, but often one of the basic causes does lie within family life. If compounded by outside weakening influences, all is lost. Parents commit sins of omission or of commission without ever realizing it. Even "black sheep" who come from God-fearing, loving parents or guardians are somehow not given the strength of character and the clear vision needed to meet the temptations and vexations of the turbulent world they have to face.

Arguments and quarrels make a home uncomfortable for a youngster. They may unfavorably condition him toward an urge for more of the same, pushing him slowly but surely toward delinquency. Counselors find that a great number of asocial children come from homes in which unstable conditions prevail. Even though parents try to conceal the true state of home life, children are not fooled.

Social workers, churchmen, teachers and members of women's clubs all have their own ideas about the causal factors of delinquency. Social workers and the clergy particularly blame parental separation and divorce. Teachers refute the tendency of parents to attribute wayward children to companionship and bad environment in and around schools. Poor or underprivileged parents say their children lack adequate supervision because both parents must be away all day working to support the family. It is true that such children are stimulated to enjoy aggression by association with undesirable playmates. In such debased areas, constant fist fights, vandalism and gang conflict provide a fertile background for augmentation of the normal aggressive impulses found in all children. Women's clubs, mostly made up of mothers, claim that television programs and theater presentations corrupt children with bloodthirsty stories depicting gangsters, desperadoes, bandits and killers as quasiheroes. Producers of such programs in turn point toward the flood of comic books and unwholesome magazines which depict beatings, shootings, stabbings, stranglings and other horrible forms of pain and death.

The good done by women's clubs is questionable if the members meet and decry juvenile delinquency, only to go home to turn on the television set and sit enthralled at some spectacle of violence and terror while their children sit near them in an ecstacy of excitement created by the conflict before them. Unknown to the mother, her children may become conditioned to identify themselves in the conflict in just that way—this is often the first step toward creating within a child the dangerous combination of love of conflict and adrenaline dependence.

The correlation between the delinquency rate and poverty does not prove anything, nor does the concentration of ethnic groups. Slums are cleared, school facilities are improved, recreational facilities are enlarged and new ones are built, more policemen are put on duty, curfews are enforced. Does delinquency disappear? It does not.

Social, religious and legal leaders often work at cross-purposes, each group going its own way in attempting to find a single cause and cure for this terrible problem of childhood. All of these people realize that today's children are tomorrow's adults. They shall inherit the world. If it is to be a better one, they must be guided into the right paths.

A leader in the crime prevention bureau of a large city has stated that society today has different moral values and mores and that the actions of today's youths are based on their interpretation of the older generation's value standards. The chief of police in another large city believes the trouble is a result of the mixture of worldwide unrest, greater educational opportunities, more money for young people to spend, more freedom and less discipline. While the educational advancements work toward a more stable and self-reliant youth, the other factors negate constructive qualities.

Patterns formed early in a child's life usually stay with him. If an aggressive type of child is faced with a dynamic conflict and a dangerous situation, he will prepare immediately for counterattack, knowing that he does not have to run away. His spirit is not broken. He stands firm to meet the challenge and in the process remains predominantly fight conditioned. Because of this kind of conditioning, he often displays the attributes of vanity and arrogance. He becomes known as a show-off.

This youngster's later life is likely to be a reflection of this fight pattern. He will preserve his acquired fight-conditioned traits and remain an extroverted aggressor who dares to do and say what he chooses. He may grow up to be any one of a great variety of individuals—boxer, wrestler, driver of racing cars, flier, mercenary soldier or perhaps even a criminal. This may seem farfetched, but a common trait runs through people of this type. Such a person will attack against great odds rather than run in the presence of danger because his positive drive is only slightly stunted by fear-conditioning. His character and approach to life are positive rather than negative.

One of the early behavioral traits of this type of aggressive child is overactivity at play—too much, too long and too hard. His parents have difficulty in making him stop playing long enough to eat the amount of food his body needs and to sleep enough for a growing child. He fights going to bed with every method he can think of, and once there he thrashes around. He refuses to take naps at a much earlier age than an average child.

With primitive fight impulses so strong, he is continually in a state of emotional tension. He is always prepared for outward attack. If it does not come, he provokes it. "Want to make something of it?" is one of his favorite questions. Again and again, he demonstrates his physiological state of an overproduction of adrenaline and its consequent overstimulation. He usually seeks more and more thrilling and dangerous kinds of play. His need for adrenaline production and satisfaction keep pace with his conflict urges, causing his dependence upon adrenaline to remain correspondingly high.

Deliberate, repeated disobedience is another danger signal. All children are disobedient at times. It is part of being a child. But the child who carries that aspect of his behavior to extremes may be heading for trouble, particularly if he shows off his worst streaks when outsiders are present. He also rebels against all those people who are in authority over him in his parents' absence—baby-sitters, nursery teachers and relatives. This deliberate rebellion against his elders may later be directed against society at large.

In addition, such a child may be spiteful and mean toward his playmates. He will go out of his way to pick a quarrel with anyone, although the degree of his positive drive will help to determine the size of the opponent he chooses. If his personality has been somewhat fear conditioned, he will start trouble with someone who is smaller and weaker than himself. Bodily conflict and the act of hurting others is pleasurable to him. Such a child needs close watching and professional help in determining why he is developing this trait of hatred. If parents can be shown in time how to condition the child favorably, it is possible to reverse undesirable tendencies.

If a parent had to choose between an introverted, delinquency-oriented child and an extroverted one, it would be a heartbreaking decision to make. Many parents have made the choice unknowingly, of course, by their little-understood conditioning powers, but that makes it none the less tragic.

The introverted child filled with hatred is only outwardly nonaggressive. Inside, his repressed emotion boils because any true expression of his feeling is blocked by fear-conditioning. He is similar to a dormant volcano upon whose sides grows a delicate grapevine. No one would guess from the placid exterior that within boils a destructive force which someday might erupt without warning in a catastrophic explosion. Usually, this kind of youngster is known by friends and acquaintances as "such a good boy." He himself seldom understands the powerful grip of the unknown force which causes him to lose control of himself. If he commits some terrible act, the papers will say he "went berserk." When questioned, the youngster may say he did it for a thrill.

The extroverted, aggressive type of young person also has a surging inward hatred, but he conceals his fight impulses poorly because his fear-conditioning is slight. He is ready to fight physically at the first opportunity. He is apt to get into situations of violence and vandalism with the full realization that they are dangerous to him. He deliberately seeks such settings for his actions so that he can satisfy his urge for action and its accompanying adrenaline flow. When this happens, the adrenaline invigorates every part of his body. In extreme cases, it becomes his reason for being.

Open conflict with a deliberately antisocial child does not pay. Often it is just what the child wants. He will willingly suffer severe punishment just for the stimulation of annoying his parents. The spanking he gets as a result of getting one or another of his parents good and mad may be well worth the physical pain it causes him.

His fearful counterpart may become an accomplished liar in order to avoid punishment. In any case, as the punishment increases in severity, so does the youngster's aggressive resistance (inward or outward). If it is inward, the child may withdraw into himself and assume an attitude of sullen hostility. A parent, noticing the sullen resentment and even hatred in his child's eyes, may pour on further punishment. This only adds fuel to the fire. Disobedience usually becomes more subtle, but it does not lessen. Parents must always be on the alert to observe stubborn aggressiveness and hostility and try to correct them before a hard-to-break habit sets in.

Once a child is recognized as a juvenile delinquent, it is most difficult to change his antisocial attitude. Most sports or other planned activities seem too tame for him. When ordered by probation officers or judges to attend planned functions with other young people his own age, he will grudgingly do so two or three times, then drop out with the comment that "it's baby stuff." To him, it is. Those dealing with such youngsters must realize that a program of slow reconditioning must be carefully planned if it is to have a chance of success. A true adrenaline dependent will experience his own peculiar type of withdrawal symptoms which must be understood and treated. It is a long process, involving a slow breaking away from the life of excitement and conflict which, in turn, lowers his adrenaline dependence.

One of the ways of dealing with such a problem child which can be successful is to turn his attention to sports, music, pets, hobbies, summer camps or vacation trips. Sometimes a combination of these interests will prove effective. Of course, they all amount to a sublimation process. If other actitivies can assume their rightful importance, dependence upon conflict and adrenaline stimulation can gradually be reduced to an acceptable level.

Without such help, an introverted youngster who harbors much hatred may think he is fulfilling his needs by joining a gang. He feels more powerful when reinforced by the combined hatred and aggressive impulses of the other members of the group. He usually identifies himself with the leader of the gang, almost always a forceful, dynamic, apparently fearless young man. He begins to dare to express his aggressions, an exhilarating sensation for him. He does not realize that all the members of the gang, many times the leader most of all, are there for the very same purpose. He would be insulted if he were compared to one of a pack of wolves—a coward alone, but an instrument of savage fury when "running" with the others.

If a child has terrible feelings of uncertainty, insecurity, danger and fearfulness and is unable to receive any help at home because of the turmoil there, he may not become gang oriented. It may be too difficult for him to get on a friendly basis with any other individual. All natural outlets for his aggressive drives are blocked, so he may become an "egger-onner," encouraging others to get into trouble because he is afraid to do so himself. Yet such a fearful child can become exceedingly dangerous if he learns the feeling of power that a gun can give him.

One of the oddities previously mentioned is the common trait that often runs through people at opposite ends of the social and economic scale. The same kind of aggressive impulses may exist, but instead of being motivated by the old, primitive, overt aggression the individual may be activated by a sublimated positive drive, even though repressed by fear-conditioning. The intellect and the imagination tap the energy and can be the source of fine creative works—writing, music or dramatic efforts, for instance.

The hypothetical life of an actor is a useful illustration. We all understand the process of identification. When we see a movie or a play with a character we admire, we sometimes "lose" ourselves in that personality. Imagination is a powerful force, one which can make an ordinary, humdrum life eventful in essence if not in actuality. The child who is destined to become an actor ordinarily exhibits a rapidly expanding aggressive drive which is not granted full expression because of frustration caused by parents or modern conditions in general. Of course, all youthfully imaginative children do not become actors, but the basic structure is there.

Strong imagination was at work in the case of the six-year-old boy who did not come to the dinner table one evening. He was discovered perched high in a tree in the backyard. His mother stood at the bottom and begged him to come down. The child merely gazed into the distance and pretended not to hear. At last, his mother gave up and went inside. After dark, the boy climbed down and went into the house and to bed. The father and mother agreed not to make a big thing of the incident, a wise decision on their part. But in the light of the following morning, the father could not resist asking a question.

"Well, son," he said, "did you have a good time last night pretending you were a bird?"

The boy was insulted and quickly answered, *"Pretending* I was a bird? Why, I *was* a bird!"

Similarly, a great actor at maturity is possessed of the faculty for becoming the person he is playing. Once, after the well-known actor Edwin Thomas Booth had given his fine performance of King Lear, an admirer unwittingly asked a touchy question.

"What is the secret of your skillful rendition of this king?" he said.

"Sir, I *am* King Lear," Booth responded with abruptness. physiologically equipped to experience the identification process to the ultimate degree. His neuroendocrine system was habituated to getting him into the mood for the "inner creative state" so vital to an actor. He could easily lose himself in the character he portrayed. Such power of complete camouflage takes years of conditioning to achieve.

Can any of us wonder that successful actors are oversensitive to stimulation from conflict in the outside world? They respond to day-to-day conflicts in the same manner in which they meet the imagined conflicts of a script. An accomplished actor may attempt to put up an antisocial barrier toward friends and acquaintances. If he is successful, his reward is a sense of peace. He succeeds in blocking stimuli from his environment. Emotional turmoil ceases to be, except for the playacting kind, which is what is craved and needed by his personality. In essence, he builds himself an imaginary cocoon which admits only well-screened stimuli.

To retain emotional stability, it is almost a necessity for some actors and actresses to surround themselves with this invisible protection. They understand their particular limits of stimulation. Controlling some aspects of outer influences is, in a sense, almost a survival measure for them. One actor put the feeling in words, set down here as well as can be remembered. "If I go into a room where there are a hundred people milling about and one of them doesn't like me, I'll sense it, and I'll have to get out of there," he said. This demonstrates more clearly than a battery of scientific opinions just how finely tuned an actor can become to stimuli and to what extent he will go to avoid those which are not to his liking.

It may seem out of place to discuss the peculiar problems of actors in a chapter dealing with juvenile delinquency. But it must be made plain that there is a definite similarity in conditioning as well as in personality structure. Successful actors are able to channel their drives into constructive outlets. The same type of person, unable to attain recognition in that field, might become a social problem. Further exploration reveals that the best-intentioned efforts of an actor can adversely affect young people watching the artistry unfolding before them, whether on a movie or a television screen or in the form of "live" theater. An audience identifies with an actor who is enduring suffering (recipient identification). If predominantly fight conditioned, a spectator identifies with an actor who is inflicting pain or distress upon another (author identification). In the former situation, the spectator takes a passive, negative role and may actually leave the theater, unable to deal with his own distress. In the latter, the spectator assumes a positive role and, in his imagination, enters into the conflict as an aggressor. Members of the audience may change their identification from one actor to another, depending on the relative intensity of danger in the conflict portrayed. As the fortunes of conflict come and go before their eyes, watchers may change their identification in conformance with their own conditioned behavioral patterns.

CinemaScope, Cinerama and other techniques used for grouping an audience about the playactors, as in the relatively new "theater in the round," draw observers more closely into the stage action. They can clearly see facial expressions, hear every word without distortion and in every way be brought into such close contact with the players that the inherent danger of the conflict portrayed is intensified.

Thus, as "culture" becomes more widely available to the

general public, little-suspected dangers inherent in it become more prevalent. Audiences are no longer satisfied with crude efforts. They are able to discern fine acting when they see it. It follows naturally that perceptive observers demand superior drama and its portrayal. The level of required stimulation for both actors and watchers increases, along with the dangers. The idea has been advanced that every force for good has elements of evil lurking within it. In this case at least, that theory is not without merit.

The children of actors face intensified danger unless they are especially protected by parents aware of the threat or unless they are able to develop the mechanism for success mastered by the adults around them. It is difficult for them to avoid early training in playacting with scripts and themes being so much a part of the family life. Added to the conflict in real life, such exposure can condition a child until during his childhood he becomes habituated to and dependent on a level of adrenaline stimulation second only to that of a soldier on the battlefield.

Such children may engage in flights of fantasy and daydream a lot. Or they may take the alternate route of overt expression and bang their heads on the floor when frustrated or throw tantrums to get their way. They may actually enjoy the distress they cause their parents. When older, they may delight in playing practical jokes and pranks or in breaking their own or other people's possessions. If they lean toward acting themselves, their early years may be characterized by chronic disobedience, antagonistic attitudes and overaggressiveness at play. Whatever form their traits of childish conflict take, they are most likely to be more intense than those experienced by other children of similar age.

None of the foregoing discussion is meant to be construed as an argument that potential actors or children of actors stand a good chance of becoming juvenile delinquents. What is being ferreted out and presented is the striking similarity in conditioning and the wide variance of behavior in later life. Some of the answers, it would appear, lie in the channeling of drives and aggressions.

The more pressing the need a young person has for the invigorating effects of fear and anger, the more important becomes the manner in which he handles that need. Acting is only one of the acceptable ways open to a talented person. Others will be discussed later, but their impact upon the public is far less familiar. Their pursuits and achievements are not flashed before countless eyes again and again. Their fame follows narrower pathways and their lives do not touch others in the same manner.

Those children who have an overpowering dependence upon excitement and the resulting flow of adrenaline have to be reconditioned much as a drug addict or an alcoholic must be rehabilitated in order to be a useful member of society. Wealthy parents sometimes attempt to solve the problem by shipping a delinquent boy off to a military school, hoping that the discipline and relatively quiet, orderly atmosphere will do the job. In some cases, it works. In others, the parents merely transfer the burden to other shoulders and make the boy feel more rejected in the process.

Carefully planned schools for delinquents have had some success. California, for instance, has proved itself noteworthy by establishing a number of forest camps where delinquent boys are slowly withdrawn from the life of overstimulation and are later returned to society with no more than normal urges for conflict and the consumption of adrenaline. The serenity of the setting must be given its share of the credit. Who could hear the wind soughing through tall trees and feel the enormity of mountain darkness without being lulled to a certain extent?

However, the prevention rather than the cure of delinquency is the real answer. It will require a widespread education of the public which so far has hardly been approached. A beginning has been made, and it is up to each one of us—whether we are parents or not—to see that no effort or expense is spared to keep delinquency from grasping our young people. Once it has taken hold, the prying-loose procedure is a long and costly one.

We have spoken of the juvenile delinquent as though such a child were always a boy. That is far from true. Girls are generally more protected in the home until an older age and therefore get a later start in delinquency than boys, but their fall from grace, once they become "wild," is more rapid and their reclamation often hopeless. A girl who gets into trouble with the law is suspected by the public of having "gone the limit" sexually. Often, that is not true, but it makes little difference in the minds of those who presume to judge her.

Girls who go this route have the same greed for excitement as boys. One ingredient which they usually lack is daring, so when they get picked up by the law they are often in the company of a gang of boys. All-girl gangs are rare. They look to boys for leadership and a measure of protection. When they add sexual relations to their already irregular lives, it is partly because the boys expect it and partly because they know they will be considered guilty anyway.

It is a shame in our so-called enlightened age that less effort is made to rehabilitate a delinquent girl than her male counterpart. Confining her in an institution with other delinquent girls is not likely to be helpful. Putting her on probation does little good, for she is rejected by the public and sometimes even by those who should still love her. These hard facts explain her diminished chances for cure.

The increased bewilderment of parents is a side effect of delinquency. As their self-confidence disappears, some of them seek a physician's help because they feel they have failed to guide their children properly. They fear a breakdown for themselves because of their extreme nervous anxiety about their young ones. Many parents dare not go to sleep at night until an unpredictable child comes home. They jump when the telephone rings for fear it may be bad news. They feel deeply shamed when their premonitions come true and their children run afoul of the law.

It is not possible to hold a child legally responsible for his misdeeds until he is able to determine the difference between right and wrong. A child's conception of these terms should be learned at his parents' knees and in the religious training which it is their duty to see that he gets. His language, customs, recreations and morals are developed in the home. Even though some parents may suffer from the same hunger for violence and adrenaline stimulation, thus serving only as models for the child to imitate, they are morally and legally responsible for that child.

The wide scope of public education needed becomes evident when we realize that the moral climate of entire communities must be lifted to eradicate objectionable adult behavior when it is the only example some impressionable adolescents have to follow. Senator Robert C. Hendrickson has pointed out that, although there is no way to enact the Golden Rule into law, it is desperately needed in our struggle against delinquency. We cannot expect to tolerate examples of hatred, greed, corruption and crass materialism, then expect children to overcome them by living up to ideals that receive only lip service from some adults. Only as each of us puts these ideals into practice will our moral and spiritual climate improve.

It is clear that delinquency is the product of many interlaced factors. The answer to the total problem will also be one of many parts. Some of those pieces of the puzzle will involve changes in attitudes and behavioral patterns by both parents and children. Coming to terms with adrenaline dependence will require a scientific knowledge of the innermost workings of the human body, a subject of little interest to many adults. Some feel that there is something indecent about discussing the physiology of digestion, excretion, reproduction. Their religious beliefs or certain other prejudices may oppose the idea that some part of the human body may influence basic behavior.

It is the acceptance of precisely such a premise that may lead to the solution to delinquency. We must recognize the fact that an urge for conflict can produce the pleasant stimulation of a sudden supply of adrenaline in the body. If urges for conflict are repeatedly gratified in objectionable ways, more and more adrenaline can become necessary in order for the body to reach the same level of stimulation. On the other hand, if the basic urge for conflict is constantly denied, frustration and hatred can follow and provoke misbehavior or even crime. But if parents are sometimes caught in the same adrenaline "traps" as their children, how can they be shown the way to help their youngsters? It is indeed a narrow tightrope we walk in our attempt to find workable solutions to the many-sided problem of delinquency.

6

The Sad State of Sadism

THE urge to derive satisfaction from inflicting unnecessary pain or suffering upon another is one of the most tragic enigmas of the human personality. All sorts of explanations have been given by every kind of person from layman to behavioral scientist. Like a delinquent, a sadist is made that way by certain combinations of events and circumstances.

Cruelty in early childhood is the flag of danger to the observant parent who is alert to the possibility of underlying sadism. A youngster who pulls the wings off butterflies and the legs off houseflies is in need of immediate and understanding help. When flypaper was widely used in bygone days, a budding sadist was easily spotted as he watched in rapt fascination the frantic struggles of the flies caught on it. Catching grasshoppers and mutilating them is still a popular sport with this type of child. If the tendency is not stopped in the right way, such a child will go right on, graduating to larger animals—chickens, birds, turtles, kittens and puppies—as he himself grows larger. Unless dealt with properly, this morbid habit is certain to expand later into pleasure at seeing other human beings suffer.

As soon as the first suspicion of sadism enters a parent's mind, he should explain to the child the vast difference between swatting a disease-carrying fly and killing a harmless butterfly. He should be taught why it is all right to kill a mosquito to end its biting spree and at the same time wrong to deliberately step on a harmless insect which may protect human life by eating germs.

55

Even an inordinate amount of deliberate toy breakage or a child's frequent refusal to eat or go to bed may be a tip-off. Disobedience which is often repeated, seemingly with the express intent of annoying parents, should alert them to watch for small acts of cruelty. If a pattern seems to be forming, professional help should be sought immediately. The earlier such tendencies are interrupted and reversed, the better the chance for complete recovery.

A child can continue secretly to be a sadist after he is stopped by one means or another from performing acts of cruelty. Strong parental disapproval may be the deterrent. Or he might try sadistic behavior on the wrong animal or on another aggressive child and be met with unexpected retaliation. If the latter happens often enough, he becomes fear conditioned and learns that the safe way to get the desired stimulation is to watch others inflict cruelty.

Some authorities contend that the existence of so many war toys—guns, tanks, battleships, rockets—brings out sadistic tendencies which might otherwise lie dormant in children who are on the borderline. Violence is so much a part of modern life that it becomes difficult to draw a line between possibly dangerous influences and the need to expose children to reality, unpleasant though some of it may be.

Workbooks allegedly containing a pattern of overt violence were used in a California fourth-grade class for more than a year before any parents complained. The illustrations included several of a woman slapping a man, a man hitting another man on the jaw, a boy sticking a dart into the hand of another youngster; and the written text contained a reference to getting a gun and the use of the word "cop" rather than "policeman." The publishers of the book defended it as being far less violence oriented than reading materials common to the parents' generation. It must be admitted that many of the classics in stories for children are brimming with cruelty and destruction; yet they are regarded with reverence and faithfully purchased for children by adults suffering from severe cases of nostalgia. The modern workbook is said to have been designed to carry a message against violence and to point up American ideals. Five million are estimated to be in use throughout the United States, with only one other recorded complaint. At last notice, the fate of the book was still hanging in the balance in California.

To be fair, critics of reading matter for children should closely examine some of our time-honored comic strips. Many of them are anything but comical. Who can calculate how many sadists loving parents may have launched by reading the "funnies" to children until they were old enough to read them alone? Before the accusing finger is pointed in any one direction, all aspects of family life must be thoroughly analyzed. The area is enormous; the burden of guilt may be more evenly distributed than any of us likes to think.

The line between sadism and pure crime is not easily drawn. The deciding factor is usually the amount of thrill that accompanies the act. Crime is often carried out for the purpose of financial gain. In true sadism, the "kicks" outweigh everything else.

One of the most shocking cases of sadism took place in New Zealand not long ago. Two 16-year-old girls beat the mother of one of them to death with a brick wrapped in a stocking. They wanted to emigrate to the United States, but the mother stood in their way. The girls decided that elimination was necessary. From what was revealed at first, their act seemed to have been criminal, but entries found later in a diary prove it to have been a sadistic killing. The girls gloried in the anticipation of their plan. Here are some of the entries from the diary:

> We are both thrilled with the idea. . . . Why couldn't Mother die? Thousands are dying daily, so why not Mother? . . . Naturally, we feel a trifle nervous, but the pleasure of anticipation is very great. . . We have decided to use a rock in a stocking rather than a sandbag. We discussed the murder fully. The happy

event is to take place tomorrow afternoon. The next time I write in my diary, Mother will be dead. How odd, yet how pleasant!

The following day's entry began as follows:

Day of a happy event. Felt very excited and night-before-Christmasy last night. Didn't have pleasant dreams, though.

The only hint of humaneness in the daughter's makeup was in the reference to unpleasant dreams. Otherwise, the whole incident appears to have been a joyous experience for the girls. After the mother's death, they ran to a nearby tearoom and said she had slipped on a plank and hit her head.

Insanity was advanced as a possible reason for their actions, but the diary entries showed without doubt that the murder was premeditated, planned with great precision. The gloating over the prospective kill furnished specific evidence of dependence upon conflict and its consequent adrenaline stimulation.

Teenage crime waves are fairly common in most large cities. Some time ago in New York City, four boys aged 15, 16, 17 and 18 went on a 16-day rampage and killed, beat and tortured victims for the fun of it. During that short span of time, they beat an old man to death, beat several other elderly men, horse-whipped two teenage girls, tied gasoline-soaked cotton around a man's legs and set it on fire and dragged another man seven blocks to dump him in the East River, where he drowned.

"It was a supreme adventure," one of the boys said later in describing their atrocities.

"I did it for sheer enjoyment," another said.

"I used them for punching bags to see how hard I could punch," a third offered as the only explanation for his actions.

Were these instances of unnecessary cruelty caused by poverty? No, because not a single victim was robbed. Neglect?

All the boys came from good homes. They belonged to the old, respected element of the city. Ignorance? All had good school records. Organized crime? None belonged to hoodlum gangs. Indeed, three of the four had been summer camp counselors in partial charge of younger children. All of them liked athletics, played competitive games, went swimming at neighborhood pools and enjoyed books and music. In these, as in other sadistic orgies, no obvious explanation was available. Without doubt, the most important causative factor was the craving for thrills produced by intense stimulation through violent conflict.

Although it is hard for many of us to understand, most juvenile vandals make no effort to hide the fact that they do terrible things just for the fun of it. Several church interiors in a Kentucky city were wantonly destroyed. In a childish scrawl on one of the walls was left this message in crayon: "We wreck just for excitement."

Obviously, these tendencies have to be reversed long before the acts themselves are accomplished if the children are to be rehabilitated without a lasting sense of guilt, which is a self-destroying emotion. The question is not *when* but *how* to start. Many times, great movements begin in small ways. Educators in general understand the need for humaneness, but too few take positive measures toward teaching it. From Los Angeles, California, comes a novel idea. It is an organization called "The Kindness Club" and it is based on the belief that a child must first learn how to treat small animals and creatures before he can learn to be truly kind to other human beings. These clubs are beginning to spread through the school system, with attendance on a purely voluntary basis. A few have put on assemblies with speakers. Some concerned mothers have started clubs at their homes. Small as this effort is in comparison to the great need, it is a start, and other cities and towns would do well to emulate the example.

Once a sadist reaches adulthood, there is not much hope for his reclamation. His need for violence and its accompanying adrenaline stimulation are too firmly entrenched in his personality. His habits have become as hardened as concrete and almost as difficult to remold.

Man's bloodthirsty inhumanity to man is not always overt. And it often extends into the so-called "normal" sector of our society. For instance, contractors claim that when their men are tearing down an old building they work with speed and enthusiasm, but when these same men are constructing a building they are slow and must be urged along by the foreman. Of course, this is the destruction of objects, not people, but there are disturbing similarities in the basic eagerness which prompts the act.

Some years ago, the Toledo Air Race attracted the largest attendance at any entertainment event ever held in this country up to that time. A crowd estimated at one and a half million watched spellbound as seven men were killed in the daring air escapades. The same fascination with injury and possible death is evident in crowds watching circus acrobats, human "flies" ascending steeples and tall buildings and the annual Memorial Day motor races at Indianapolis. These danger-fraught events are reminiscent of the ancient Roman Coliseum spectacles.

In viewing rather than inflicting cruelty, observer identification takes place. In Mexico, Portugal, Spain, Central America and South America, the bullfight fan cheers his favorite toreador, feeling as though he himself were down there in the ring fighting for his life against the maddened bull. Identification actively occurs in front of televisions which show deadly gun battles and mauling hand-to-hand fights between men in a rage. Such things are evidently not painful or disagreeable to normal people or they would not survive as mediums of entertainment. All this carries a disturbing implication.

Just as it is much more enjoyable and satisfying to eat a confection rather than merely to look at it, so must it be more stimulating for some people to engage in hurting others rather than watching from a safe distance. But the fact that either method pleases society, even in isolated cases, is a nightmare that will continue to haunt behavioral scientists for a long time to come unless every known fact about the human body's effect upon itself is squarely studied and searched for solutions. The neuroendocrine mechanism already discussed is capable of provoking pleasurable stimulation by strange means. The answer to a major portion of society's puzzling problems lies there, waiting for acceptance and corrective action.

No universally acceptable explanation has been given for sadism since the original investigations of the Marquis de Sade. He depicted the trait as a sexual perversion in which gratification is obtained by torturing the loved person. The concept has subsequently undergone modification to mean the love of cruelty conceived as a manifestation of sexual desire. A recent play on the subject involving the Count has filled theaters to overflowing and made sadism a fashionable subject of conversation.

Exception must be taken to any tendency to ascribe sadism exclusively to sexual roots. For that to be true, sex would have to govern some aspects of human behavior completely unrelated to it. It would mean assigning sexual sources for the energy of aggressive impulses. Although sexual and aggressive processes are recognized as bearing a physiological relationship within the body, the related urges are fundamentally different in function and structure. The sexual urge is directed toward propagation and the sex glands; the aggressive urge is directed toward the preservation of the present generation and the adrenal glands. It is true that conflict involving sex is part of the picture of conflict in general. But sadism is a broad concept dealing with cruelty in general and having sexual implications only insofar as conflict is involved with sex. It is the product of a basic, inborn, aggressive drive which, because of the conditioning of the individual, is released directly as cruelty rather than sublimated and released indirectly through sports and good works. The true sadist is conditioned to the pleasurable thrill of his violent exploits. The stimulation he receives from harming others is caused by the action of chains of reciprocal reflexes which are aroused just as automatically as are cough and swallow reflexes. After a pattern like this is set, even great willpower often cannot break the habit. Even though sadists may be caught and eliminated from free society by prison sentences, they have achieved a pinnacle of attention which thrills them and makes any punishment worth enduring.

It does not seem natural to associate sadism with sociability; yet an individual so conditioned does not want to be alone. He must be a social being in order to engage in conflictive situations which provide the stimulation so necessary to him. This is one of the tragedies of extreme adrenaline dependence—it can be satisfied only by inflicting suffering or humiliation upon a fellow human being. It does not seem to matter to the offending individual that he makes himself less and less welcome as the hateful aspects of his personality are necessarily revealed to others.

Very recently, a pensioner made a late-evening trip downstairs for cigarettes available in the lobby of this rooming house. As he entered the elevator to go back upstairs, a man to whom he paid little attention held the elevator door open for him. The stranger got out on the same floor and followed the elderly man to his room. Once inside, he knocked him down, beat him and took twelve dollars from his wallet. As if that weren't enough, before he left he squirted lighter fluid on the old man and lit it. Someone from across the hall came in and put out the fire after the assailant left. The pensioner was not expected to live.

It is difficult for the average person to understand how a country like ours, which strives for the best advantages for all, can produce sadistic monsters who roam throughout every section of the land and every segment of society.

Most informed readers are familiar with the incident involving several Marines who killed five Vietnamese civilians. This is shocking to us partly because we have been conditioned to expect this sort of thing from the Viet Cong but not from our own servicemen. The full story may never be unraveled, but one Marine is serving a life sentence and the others lesser lengths of time. It may be that theirs was not a case of true sadism, although one of the Marines was reported to have laughed as he participated in the killings. It is a fact that war brutalizes men, and the slayings in Vietnam may have been an instance of pent-up hostility exploding, a different phenomenon. We do not know.

It remains the task of medical researchers and other scientists to examine every bodily process, particularly those involving the production of and demand for excessive adrenaline. The answer to many social ills may be within reach.

7

The Criminal

*He who is bent on doing evil
can never want occasion.*
PUBLILIUS SYRUS

THE general term "criminals" includes kleptomaniacs, hit-and-run drivers, arsonists, pickpockets, house robbers, holdup men, sex offenders, kidnappers and killers. In varying degrees, each suffers from the same afflication, an insatiable urge to be a nonconformist, to run counter to the established order. Each one knows that if he is apprehended and convicted he will pay the penalty prescribed by law; yet that knowledge does not deter him because his urge is stronger by far than his fear.

True criminals get that way by becoming conditioned to daily conflicts which cause their body fluids to be constantly forced out of chemical balance through a craving for excessive stimulation. From a physiological standpoint, such a person is as ill as the alcoholic who cannot get through a day without a drink. Instead of one or many drinks, this person seeks out conflicts which carry extreme danger. He is given to periods of great rage and may attack anyone with fists or the nearest weapon for no other reason than the "kicks" he must have.

As a child, he was undoubtedly fight conditioned to a great degree. His acquired dependence upon conflict and adrenaline dates back beyond his earliest memories. He grows up with the name of being "a born scrapper" and everybody who knows him tries to keep out of his way. Poor environment is almost a certain element of his early life. His hatred and hostility toward the world at large led him into juvenile delinquency, which he quickly left behind in favor of more vicious pursuits. In adulthood, he becomes an extremely dangerous person because the slightest provocation may arouse him to violent rage. The adrenal glands, in an orgasm similar to sexual orgasm, produce a sudden gush of adrenaline, followed by an immediate exhilaration of the ego and the extinction of his sense of pity. This, in turn, leads to the loss of all fear of the consequences of his act, so he is able to commit a heinous crime. Relatives and neighbors are usually unable to explain his conduct. The victim may have been his own mother who chided him in the way of most mothers. After it is too late, he may weepingly declare that he loved her.

The behavior of such a person may seem to be that of a crazy man. This is a misconception. He is not crazy. He is a cunning, shrewd individual who knows what he wants in the way of stimulation and knows how to get it. His urge to conflict seethes within and tolerates no repression.

One cannot say that poverty, bad companionship, home environment, deliberate training in crime or any other single influence drives such a person to crime. Fine families occasionally produce a "black sheep." In some underprivileged families, some of the members may become criminals while others grow up to be good citizens. Extensive studies have produced a number of conclusions, but few have sought to look within the workings of the individual's body for the cause of crime.

Pyromaniacs have puzzled criminologists and psychiatrists for many years. At one time, this compulsion to set things afire was regarded as some sort of sexual aberration because of the confessed thrill which apprehended persons readily acknowledged to investigators. It is now possible to understand that arson is an intensely pleasurable emotional experience for the pyromaniac because of his craving for the stimulation of conflict, a fact which even he may not suspect. All he knows is that the best way for him to get a thrill is to watch a self-set, destructive, dangerous fire. He releases his aggressive impulses on people he may not even know.

Investigators who can get to a fire in time know that the

culprit who set it is usually standing among the crowd of persons watching the excitement. Experienced arson investigators also know that unless the criminal is caught another fire will soon be ablaze. Few things can restrain him from repeating the thrill that he cannot obtain in any other way. Even the knowledge that human beings may be in the building often does not stop him.

Kleptomania is not a deadly crime, but it is a crime just the same. It stems from an unusual personality trait which gives the perpetrator a peculiar thrill in accomplishing the theft of property belonging to others. Usually, the stolen articles have little monetary value. Wealthy women are often caught taking small articles. It is the craving for an emotional thrill that overcomes them, one so strong that they cannot resist it. Intense shame follows any detection. Even the person involved usually does not understand the reason for the foolish action.

Sometimes the reason for a more serious crime is monetary gain. In other cases, that is only an incidental by-product of the action. Few would admit it, but the stimulation received from the display of power by pointing a gun at a victim promotes a dulling of the cortical centers of the brain, the seat of ethical and moral inhibitions. A man exhilarated under these circumstances loses his fear of the consequences and becomes highly dangerous. Also, criminals enjoy reliving their deeds of aggression against their fellow men. Considered in retrospect, the acts again excite pleasurable stimulation. The imprisoned criminal continually "chews his cud" this way and adds to it the excitement of planned revenge on those who captured and punished him.

The so-called remorse of a deliberate murderer is probably nonexistent. Of course he is sorry he was caught, but any other feelings of regret are usually dreamed up by some sentimental observer.

Society is forced to retaliate against a criminal. The first step is the detection of the aggressor. It is often aided today by the use of the polygraph, or lie detector. The criminal is unable to control an automatic inner urge to relive his actual crime in his imagination when asked questions regarding it. In so doing, the same physical changes take place in his body that occurred when he committed the crime. These bodily changes are recorded by the lie detector.

When a lie-detector test is given to determine a suspect's guilt or innocence, the subject is told that the test will show whether or not he answers the questions truthfully. If he tells the truth, he has nothing to worry about. In this way, emotional tension in the guilty person is intensified; the innocent subject is relieved. Several neutral questions are asked first, followed by pointed questions related to the crime, similar to the following:

"Is your name James Johnson?"

"What did you have for breakfast?"

"Do you like to go to the movies?"

"Did you kill Jack Bird?"

"Do you know who did it?"

"When did you go fishing last?"

"Do you know you may go to the penitentiary for what you did?"

"What other sports are you interested in?"

"Where did you bury Jack Bird's body?"

In response to each question, any changes in the rate of the suspect's pulse, blood pressure, respiration, perspiration or arm and leg motion are charted by stylus pens on a moving white paper tape. When the person lies, the pens record a significant jump in these bodily reactions. When he is asked irrelevant questions, no physical changes occur, and the pens trace a normal course.

What takes place is a series of reciprocal reflexes involving the nervous system and the body. If a guilty person is being tested, any question related to the crime produces for him the dangerous situation of detection. The danger is intensified because he is unable to control the automatic urge to relive his crime in imagination. He sees himself performing the act, but he must lie to protect himself. In response to these danger stimuli, the negative drive is vitalized and the same bodily reactions occur that follow any dangerous situation. Relaxation becomes impossible. Reflex somatic nerve messages passing from the brain to the diaphragm and skeletal muscles tend to increase respiration and cause the guilty person to crouch in his chair, an old survival reflex that enabled early man to be ready to run or to attack. Leg and arm restraining straps register this crouch. A guilty person subjected to a lie-detector test is no more able to control the urge to relive his criminal act in his imagination, his fear of detection and the resulting physical changes than is a person who unexpectedly comes upon a ferocious animal able to control his fear. In both situations, nature's response to the stimulus of danger and the resulting physical changes are automatic and beyond the control of willpower.

No long ago, criminals found that by slipping a tack into one shoe before taking the test they could confuse the persons conducting it. When an unimportant or irrelevant question is asked, the criminal presses on the tack hard enough to cause himself pain. This self-induced pain has the same results as the criminal's fear of detection during applicable questions. The confusing bodily reactions take place after both kinds of questions. Authorities have become aware of this trick and now guard against it.

A different kind of lie-detector test was used long ago in India. It was based on human physiology and was called "the ordeal of rice." Those suspected of a crime were given consecrated rice to chew. Shortly afterward, they had to spit it upon the leaf of a sacred fig tree. If a suspect ejected dry rice, it was taken as proof of his guilt. The phenomenon is explainable by the actions of adrenaline and of sympathetic nerve impulses aroused by the fear of detection, although it could not have been explained that way at the time. The fear caused the saliva to thicken and hence reduced its moistening qualities. Thus, before the dawn of the science of physiology, it was possible to connect the crime and the criminal fairly accurately.

There are not as many women criminals as men, although

the ratio is slowly changing. Women were for so long repressed that they are still more inhibited than men and refrain from giving way to their inner urges. But emotions can rage as wildly within women as within men. Decades ago, women knew that their habitually dependent position scarcely allowed for any aggressive action. They knew that a weaker woman attacking a stronger man would certainly come out the loser. And punishment for a disobedient or defiant female was severe. This dependent position of woman resulted from years of forced realization that she could not match man's physical strength, much less the emotional power which man derives from being the provider and the protector. Woman also knew that she was no match for the aggressiveness of man's fight-conditioned personality. Woman had to endure the danger and drudgery of childbearing and rearing and had never known the feelings of freedom and superiority man automatically felt. She could not protect herself from man's sexual attacks upon her. This fear-conditioned attitude resulted in almost total submission from an outward viewpoint.

Today, women are quickly becoming less fear conditioned because their rights and privileges are protected by law and by changing custom. Their status has been raised in the home, in courts, everywhere in this country. As they realize that the masculine population is daily becoming more frustrated, they tend to become more overtly aggressive. One can hardly pick up a city paper without finding somewhere in its pages the account of a wife murdering her husband or a scorned woman doing away with her ex-lover.

A lively argument rages all the time among people who try to delve into the criminal mind to find out whether or not it will always plague society. If tendencies are spotted early enough and corrective action is undertaken on a large enough scale, there is a good chance that some day a true criminal may be an oddity in our society.

8

Mr. In-Between

Every man hath a good and a bad angel
Attending on him in particular, all his life long.
ROBERT BURTON

IT is strange that many gentle, normally agressive people gather to watch a building burn down, to see a corpse brought out of a house or to see mangled bodies taken from a wrecked automobile. They will profess horror, but still they watch. Most of us are a mixture of good and evil: we are entirely human. The amount of each ingredient varies with each person, but there are few saints among the human race. Perhaps that is for the best. If there were, the rest of us could not stand comparison with a perfect example.

Even the most docile among us have subconscious urges to experience danger. We may gratify it by reading books about a variety of activities we would not be brave enough to engage in. We may sit in a darkened theater and watch actors emote so that we can do the same vicariously. We may talk glibly of our "cultural" activities; but deep underneath there is the ancient attraction for danger that our forebears knew when they first began to walk erect. We are better off being honest with ourselves. Up to a certain point, this sensation of pleasure in the presence of peril is valuable. It is nature's way of giving us courage to face danger and a good chance to survive. We would be lost—literally—without it. It is only when urges toward danger get out of hand that we are in for trouble.

There are so many degrees of aggressive tendencies that only general classifications can be set down. Some of them cannot be given the label of "good" or "bad." Is it not a tribute to man's courage that as soon as the idea of going to the moon was advanced hundreds volunteered for the trip, even though they knew there was little chance of returning alive?

We have come a long way in our thinking, in our discoveries and in our inventions. Society and personal expediency have taught us to set up a more ethical, safer world for all. But no matter how our mental processes have improved with education and progressive civilization, the old inflexible pattern of response still holds the upper hand in our emotional life. Basically, it is the same today as in the time of our primitive ancestors. We have learned to control outward manifestations of emotion, but it still churns in the viscera.

Natural aggressive tendencies are carried out in a variety of ways; some of them are hardly noticed by others, while some cause the aggressor to be regarded as a pest. As long as pettiness characterizes such acts, they stay within the limits of what is normal. An ideal illustration of such a person is the fellow who parks too close to your driveway so that you can't get your car in or out. He insists on mowing his lawn early Sunday morning. He turns on his radio or television set full blast and perhaps goes outside and doesn't even listen. If you complain, he puts you in your place by telling you that you don't own the parking space along the street and that his television set is on his own private property. If this hypothetical person is a relative, he may drop in uninvited and stay all day or all week.

Such a person cares little about your feelings. It may not occur to him even to consider them. Others get a kick out of the annoyance they cause you. Usually this type of person is careful not to go beyond petty annoyance. He will do nothing serious enough to give you an excuse to call the police. He may call you a poor sport or swear when you object to his provoking actions. He is irritating and exasperating. When one is tempted to exchange angry words with him, it is best to hold back. He may well be a pest, but he is rarely a lawbreaker.

Individuals having a strong dependence upon stimulation are the problem people of the world. The problem they present to society is in direct ratio to their degree of dependence. They may be male or female. They are to be found everywhere, even in key positions. We all occasionally come into contact with them. Much of our own lack of self-confidence arises from the uncomfortable awareness that we fail to understand the motive in back of these overt aggressors and the veiled hatred and hostility which we sense in their attitude. We try in vain to determine what we did to warrant such antagonism. Without a personal appreciation of the craving for stimulation which is characteristic of such people who are conditioned to conflict and adrenaline dependence, we cannot hope to fathom the character of the overt aggressor.

Once you are able to identify potential overt aggressors, you will readily see that when one approaches you he is usually in a combative mood. He practically dares you to knock the chip off his shoulder. He is always spoiling for a fight, and he expects you to be an accommodating fellow who will provide him with the conflict he desires without active retaliation. Even if he succeeds in tricking you into an argument, his thirst for attack will be only briefly satisfied. He is not at all interested in the facts of the argument; he will zestfully argue on either side of the question. All he wants is a conflict so that his inner works will be roused and provide the stimulation he is yearning for. If he finds that you will not argue with him and are a poor source from which to seek this stimulation, he will cease to bait you. You will become no challenge—only a bore. He may confuse you later by being agreeable instead of combative. This is his way of letting you know that, in his opinion, you are a "softie," without spunk.

Such a person is to be pitied. Because of his utter dependence upon stimulation, he is truly a slave to his passions. Even he cannot predict what he may do when aroused. His urges control him to such an extent that he may fly off the handle at an important person at the most inopportune time, perhaps even when the possibility of advancement in his business career is at stake. Because he is conscious of his lack of control, he has no self-confidence. His further distrust of himself is caused by his inability to anticipate the behavior of others. The old saying "Know thyself" is incomprehensible to him. He can know neither himself nor anyone else. He is not fitted for a job in which cooperation with other personnel is important because he cannot handle people. To work with others successfully, one must be able to influence their actions in a favorable manner.

Once you have a working knowledge of the true nature of people who are seeking to gratify an urge for overt aggression, you are in a position similar to that of the operator of a power saw. The power saw is dangerous, but the operator knows how it works, as well as how and when to turn it on and off. It can cause no trouble if handled properly. The same is true in handling an aggressor. Your insight into his trouble makes you tolerant of his weakness. You find that you are able to approach him sympathetically. Even though he is in a conflictive mood, he can sense your sympathy and respond to it because he is a highly sensitive person in spite of his strong, positive drive. If you laughingly agree when he "wisecracks" about your own deficiencies, he will probably laugh with you. You will give him a good-feeling and, at the same time, avoid conflict. If you can develop this understanding attitude toward an antagonistic person, it increases your own self-confidence immeasurably and enables you at the same time to benefit from the basically good qualities which the aggressor has.

If an overt aggressor insists on making some sort of attack on you (verbal or otherwise), he is often more friendly afterwards than before because he feels grateful to you for helping him to obtain the stimulation, although he may not realize it. However, if you show resentment or make it plain that you bear a grudge against him, he will remain unfriendly.

Charles Darwin probably gave little thought to the personalities of conflict-oriented people, but he did say that he had heard it stated that a man when excessively jaded would sometimes invent imaginary offenses and put himself in a passion for the sake or reinvigorating himself. And he added this remark to the discussion: "Since hearing this, I have occasionally recognized its full truth."

Actually, it is necessary at times for most of us to become overt aggressors to a degree because of the demands of our environment. Even in modern community life, with its emphasis on fear-conditioning, aggressive urges cannot forever be repressed or sublimated. The age-old urge to resolve conflict has a way of forcing itself to expression in order that physiological processes may be consummated and drives released. Thus even the kindly old lady has her own conditioned pattern for expressing her positive urge to conflict in word or deed, be it ever so mild and unobtrusive.

The term "normal aggressor" will be used simply because it fits most of the population. Such a person under ordinary circumstances has a good capacity for friendship and is usually affable. But at times he unknowingly derives stimulation by causing others discomfort when he is sure there is little danger of retaliation. He is moderately fear conditioned, and as a result he is only moderately aggressive. Under most circumstances, this type of individual has a good working capacity and is a middle-of-the-road kind of person. Most of the time he is considered a good fellow. He is often the champion of the underdog. He is the first to jump into deep water to save a drowning person.

From this norm, aggression goes to both extremes. The below-normal or subnormal aggressor is strongly fear conditioned. He is usually phlegmatic, difficult to arouse to wrath, gentle, patient, friendly and obliging. But, without really intending to, he can derive physiological stimulation by engaging in mild aggression when there is extremely slight danger of retaliation. But he conceals an overabundant nervous anxiety, and unless his craving for stimulation is occasionally satisfied he may kick the family pets, browbeat his wife, spank his children or even engage in fusses with kindly neighbors. However, once his infrequent craving for stimulation is satisfied, he will be very slow to take offense again.

The extroverted or vicious aggressor is prone to release his violent emotions abruptly and powerfully. He has practically no nervous anxiety and delights in seeking our conflictive situations in which great danger is present. The strong possibility of retaliation from others gives him an added thrill. He is easily roused to great anger and may become a menace to others during his periods of rage. His personality is in every way a direct contrast to that of the introverted aggressor who lives in a constant state of dread. Both totally extroverted and totally introverted aggressors are rare.

There are countless levels and degrees of aggression between the two extremes. Some of them cause great human misery, even though they are not far from the middle of the scale. The employee who dares not "bite back" for fear of losing his job may store up hatred and grudges during an emotionally exhausting day at the office, then explode at his family when he gets home. An employer may criticize his oldest and most trusted employees because they will take abuse which younger workers would not tolerate. Physicians know better than anyone else how frequent such situations are from the confiding statements of their patients. Many business establishments and homes are living hells because of an insatiable urge to conflict on the part of someone in a position of authority.

There is also the masochist, who needs self-hurt in order to excite adrenaline production for stimulation. Because of his deeply repressed and inwardly directed positive drive, his nervous system and the rest of his body are conditioned to endure self-imposed cruelty. This craving for suffering explains why many persons are social and financial failures. They expect few ventures in their lifetime to be successful. They are conditioned to failure. Actually, they would be inwardly and inexplicably upset if they suddenly became successful. Their entire physiological mechanism would be disrupted. The old saying "Put a beggar on a horse and he rides to the devil" is full of wisdom. If these people inherited money, they would play the horses, gamble at casinos or bet on anything, knowing they would probably lose, and subconsciously *wanting* to lose.

The confidence man should really be classified as a criminal, but the fact that it takes a certain kind of victim to make his scheme possible takes him out of that category for the purpose of this discussion. It has usually been assumed that the man works on the innate greed of his victims. A better explanation is that the victim is often a latent homosexual who responds to the fascination of the confidence man, who is highly conditioned to conflict and dependent on adrenaline. This dependence is gratified by directing aggressive designs toward others with the goal of getting money under false pretenses. The victim, who must have a similar dependence, is caught up in the excitement of the projected plan, so much so that he is blind to the hoax being played on him. By the time the fraud is discovered, the confidence man has usually obtained his stimulation, while the victim, who needed the same result, instead suffers an emotional hangover caused by great frustration.

Love of litigation, or an inordinate desire for battle in legal arenas, is an indication of conditioning to conflict and of adrenaline dependence as much as some of the more evident urges. This drive is simply one of the many means of aggression open to people whose need for stimulation leads them along odd pathways. One man who left his mark on legal history in the United States during the last century had thirty-six lawsuits going at the same time. In one instance, when he lost a case, he turned and sued the judge, the prosecutor, all twelve jurymen and various witnesses. He was considered a paranoid, but the truth was that he merely chose that method of satisfying his particular craving for excitation.

The person who has a persecution complex is still another kind of aggressor. He always has a grievance against someone he feels is "doing him wrong." He constantly thinks of himself as the victim of ingratitude, treachery and unkindness. Usually he blames a neighbor, relative or friend. Most people are sympathetic and consoling when they first hear his story. It sounds plausible because it contains some elements of truth.

What finally makes the most attentive listener suspicious is the great number of persons who allegedly mistreat and abuse him and the fact that he always seems to get a "raw deal."

Psychologists studying the problem of the persecution-complex personality have not reached definite conclusions regarding its causes. There is no clinical evidence of schizophrenia. Postmortem examinations never show organic lesions. At one time such behavior was thought to be a form of paranoia in which the victim suffers delusions of grandeur along with his feelings of persecution. In the absence of any talent or ambition, he can gain attention only by telling stories about his mistreatment and by generally causing trouble. His conduct compensates his ego.

It now appears that the source of his trouble is that he is conditioned to a high level of dependence on conflict and adrenaline stimulation. His required amount of hormone rises to such a point that he must disturb, irritate and prod others until outright conflict is finally produced. When he first tells his story of mistreatment, he is surprisingly friendly, calm and innocent acting. This is disarming to the listener and occurs because he is grateful to the present audience for its attentiveness and for allowing him to relate his often-repeated troubles and conflicts. While relating these events, he relives them in his imagination until he himself hardly remembers which is fact and which is fiction. He relates incidents convincingly. Thus he derives pleasurable stimulation by expressing his feelings of repressed hatred for those who supposedly mistreated him.

The listener, though, finds that after this type of person has exhausted his tales of hating others he may begin to do mean and humiliating things to his confidant. He may even become physically menacing. The person attacked by such an individual wonders what he did to cause provocation. He did nothing. The original pleasant attitude of this aggressor changed to obnoxiousness when he exhausted his stories about others and was forced by his urges to redirect his hatred toward his unlucky listener and to attack him as the most convenient target. Such a slave to stimulation has a compulsion to get it by any means. It is obviously best to avoid a persecution-motivated person, for his unsatisfied conflict and adrenaline hunger may even drive him into a murderous rage.

It is easy to see that the wise handling of human aggression is one of the major challenges of our time. In fact, when one thinks of the steadily swelling world population, it becomes evident that a swift and wise solution is imperative to our survival as a species.

9

No Place to Hide

And blood in torrents pour
In vain—always in vain,
For war breeds war again.
JOHN DAVIDSON

ALTHOUGH man's emotional reactions are almost four hundred generations removed from the Old Stone Age, the fears, hatred and violence of the squatting place and the cave still bear their bitter fruit today in the primitive conditioning of man's intellect and reactions to the waging of war.

War is and has always been the greatest problem of mankind. Man must understand the psychology of war, its causes and effects, if he is to understand himself. Like all mysterious and unknown forces, the threat of war is attended by a powerful dread, for no one has been able to explain with any completeness its underlying causes. Lack of self-confidence among members of the human race has caused a recurring, haunting fear of war. It is a spectre which lingers always on the fringes of our consciousness. We are never really rid of it. Even when other affairs are going well, the threat of war keeps us from relaxing. We must study this combined, collective type of aggression and strip it, layer by layer, of its components if we are to understand its causes and to formulate effective ways of eliminating them.

In the past, war was usually a personal issue for those on the battlefield. Today, things are different. The life of every man, woman and child in the world is touched directly or indirectly at some time by this scourge, and strife between nations and ideologies has become both a universal and a personal problem. A large majority of the adults living today have come through two world wars and live in constant terror of a third, more devastating conflict. The atom bomb, the long-range jet plane, the intercontinental ballistic missile and the nuclear-powered submarine have brought the threat of war frighteningly close to every living person, no matter where he is. Even the race to reach nearby planets is coupled with the fear that their possession will provide additional means for waging a totally destructive war. We are afraid to pause in our frantic race for fear another nation will get ahead of us. Advanced scientific knowledge in nervous hands can trigger some impulsive action that will quickly thrust us past the point of no return. Frightened man no longer has a place in which to run and hide.

As we look back, even the most constructive inventions worsened the threat of war. The steam engine made it possible for huge battleships to prowl the oceans of the world with their awesome armaments. It was simple, too, for rail transportation to shift larger armies of men more swiftly than ever before. Gasoline made possible armored cars, airplanes, submarines and tanks. Heavy artillery, machine guns, atomic weapons and intercontinental ballistic missiles followed in thundering sequence. Activities directly related to war spread to large segments of the population. The interests of the workers involved paralleled in great part the interests of the military.

At the beginning of the twentieth century, military might dealt with individuals—usually one enemy at the business end of a rifle, bayonet or sword. Later, the machine gun killed dozens. Then heavy artillery rained death on hundreds. At the start of World War II, aerial bombs destroyed thousands. Later in the same war, the perfected atom bomb destroyed hundreds of thousands. Since then, improvements in electronics and other scientific processes have made the devastation of the world as we know it a distinct possibility. Man's stepped-up urge to conflict and his desire for greater adrenaline stimulation have whetted his craving until the ability to kill one human being at a time will no longer satisfy him.

Leslie Weatherhead puts it well in his *Psychology, Religion and Healing:*

> Man has released the energies of the physical world until they terrify him. He has created a Frankenstein monster that has wrecked his nerves and paralyzed his brain with fear. Power has been released but man lacks the wisdom to use it. One illustration suffices. The natives of Bikini would supply it. A power released by alien scientists drove them from the island home where they and their ancestors had resided for centuries, but no one knows how to end the harm which that release has effected. The 'djinn' released one summer day has poisoned the very sea and still lurks in its depths with a horror called radioactivity, incomprehensible to them. No one knows how to drive the 'djinn' back into its bottle and old Father Time—on whom alone reliance is placed—is in no hurry. At the point at which man has unleashed unrivaled power he is most hopeless. Never has he handled such power. Never has he been so frightened and uncertain.

Today, the testing of atomic weapons and intercontinental missiles is going on in many parts of the world. Man races against man in devising the swiftest, farthest reaching and most deadly weapon. This race creates a worldwide fear which is highly explosive. An awareness of danger by a predominantly fear-conditioned people is always accompanied by fear-producing hatred, anger and aggressiveness. Many tyrants since Alexander's time have learned to their sorrow the folly and cost of awakening fear in others.

As nations plunge into war, the level of brutality, violence and murder builds up until one nation is finally brought to its knees in abject surrender. There follows an immediate emotional hangover for the vanquished and a delayed hangover of the same kind for the victor until, through reconditioning, each returns in time to the sustaining intensity of conflict and the level of dependence on adrenaline which existed before the tension became unbearable. Thus the conflictive cycle is complete, having lain dormant between nations until it was inexorably fanned again by danger, fear, hatred and adrenaline overstimulation.

Each cycle adds new perfections to the art of torture. Warfare has widened its locale from the battlefield to every conceivable spot on earth. Undoubtedly, at this very moment, many nations have medical scientists hard at work hurrying to be the first to perfect and stockpile the latest "Pandora's box" or horror for the next great conflict. Germ warfare is one of the most terrifying threats held over the head of mankind for a long time. Just when medical advances have almost wiped some of the great scourges from the earth, the tide is being reversed and these same diseases now wait just offstage to be loosed on innocent men, women and children once more! The fact that deadly germs could be spread by airplanes or secretly put into water supplies for cities makes it the kind of warfare that no line of defense could hold back. Destruction has many faces. Any one of them serves to demonstrate how precariously we tread.

As a great part of the working population of nations becomes more directly involved with the military by providing the implements of war, those people naturally feel a quickening of the sense of danger and of fear and hatred. They reason thus: if there were not danger of similar weapons being used against them and a need for retaliation, why would they be devoting large portions of their lives to perfecting such instruments?

What would be considered criminality on an individual basis slowly becomes legal on a mass scale. More than that, it comes to be thought of as an absolute necessity. The major parts of many national economies are based on the threat of war. The cartoons and clever columns written with the theme of "What would we do if *peace* should strike?" are not as humorous as they are intended to be. There is a core of grim and sober truth in them.

A swing from the negative drive to the positive drive in a

predominantly fear-conditioned society is the usual pattern of building up to war hysteria. War engendered by fear and hatred is as old as the gathering together of early men for protection. From fear springs all the progressive passions and primitive emotions that terminate in warfare. Populations have always suffered from the fears of invasion, of siege, of starvation by blockage, of the death of loved ones, of loss of property, of being led away to enslavement, and a host of other fears which are conjured up by the imagination and constantly end in the horror of a reality at war.

One of the most dynamic manifestations of hatred is present in war, for it is there that all the inherent savagery and wickedness of man comes to the surface. Brutality and murder are condoned by the populace. Burning and pillage are accepted, and enslavement and rape are common, even in modern warfare. In war, it becomes especially difficult to separate the "good guys" from the "bad guys." A man with a temperament prone to hatred is ready to see life in terms of vindictive melodrama. He is prepared to find his needed stimulus and satisfaction in frightful demonstrations of revenge and so-called "justice." The candid observer can see in victor and vanquished alike the true primitive aggressiveness of the human personality.

The study of warfare shows that, when combat summons up the powerful bodily mechanisms that warriors must have in order to survive, men who were once considerate and kind become infuriated savages. They slaughter women and children, mutilate the defenseless, burn, ravish and loot. They appear to be mad or under the influence of some powerful drug. They are neither mad nor artificially drugged—they are transported by the utmost release of aggressive impulses and they act in the white-hot fervor of the moment. All sense of morality and pity is swept aside by their emotional intoxication. They lose completely their sense of mercy.

This intense craving for pleasurable stimulation is the most vicious state of existence known to man. When hand-to-hand combat is a feature of warfare, participants often suffer a withdrawal syndrome when they are taken from the arena of battle. By military custom, soldiers who have been on the battlefield for some time and have engaged in daily physical attacks upon the enemy are periodically removed to a quiet area for rest and regrouping. It is then that some exhibit withdrawal symptoms similar to those experienced by alcoholics under treatment. They may have a looseness of the bowels, alternate sweats and chills, restlessness, extreme anxiety, apprehension and sleeplessness.

Strangely, some feel an irresistible urge to return to the battle lines they have just left. Occasionally, they will say they feel as though their dead buddies are calling to them to come back. Little do they realize that it is their deeply conditioned physiological need for emotional stimulation that is urging them to renew combat at the front. Soldiers safely behind the front lines often toss around in their bunks, irritable and full of complaints, until roused by the magic words, "The push is on!"

The fact that so many students at West Point are the sons of officers carries out the contention that early life on military posts exerts strong conditioning effects of children. As the Mayo brothers tagged after their father and became so conditioned to a medical career that no other life appealed to them, so officers' sons absorb their childhood surroundings. The fact that the end results are so widely divergent has nothing to do with the conditioning forces. Officers can take a studious, shy private and turn him into a savage fighting machine. A quiet, even-tempered, kindly person can become cruel, mean and vindictive if his training molds him in that manner.

Learned behavior in modern life is dependent on the fact that transgressions of social dictates are promptly followed by a retaliation of organized forces. Under these circumstances, the positive urges of most people are submerged in time by inexorably fearful responses to almost all dangers encountered. Human behavior is dominated by fear-conditioned reflexes, so called because their establishment is conditional upon many past circumstances of attack and frustration. These individual reflexes, elaborated after birth and dependent to a great extend on continuing education and training, are also spoken of as temporary associations because they can be eliminated by actively practicing aggression. But when the practice of active aggression dismisses fear-conditioning for a period of time, it will reappear when proper conditions are reestablished, and with less effort than was needed the first time.

Need it be explained further why shipwrecked sailors and passengers drifting helplessly at sea in a small boat, or landed on a cramped and barren island, are prone to war upon one another? It is not only the thirst for fresh water and a need for sufficient food but also thirst and hunger for excitation that bothers them. Thus tiny wars and enormous ones spring from a common seed. A famous arctic explorer once explained that he preferred to pass winter months in frozen lands alone because he knew that if he had companions they would eventually be at one another's throats.

Many theories for the cause of wars have been advanced and some still have avid supporters. It is easy to punch holes in each doctrine as the basic, sole cause by pointing out exceptions to it.

Marx's theory of economic determinism places the cause of war on the clashing of nations seeking access to a continuous supply of raw materials and the conquest of new areas in which to sell and distribute finished manufactured products. If his theory is to hold water, the American Indians should have been living in peace when the white man first came to America because they had enormous areas to spread outward and into for purposes of barter or any other objectives they could have had in mind. But they were not living in peace. They were engaged in a state of incessant warfare, attacking, murdering and pillaging.

Believers in the theory of nationalism charge that self-centered nations struggle constantly for the enlargement of their frontiers. They cite that a succession of national wars has taken place since early historical times—Greeks and Trojans, Greeks and Persians, Romans and Carthaginians and so on.

Redress for former wrongs is given as the spark which ignites such wars. However, in the United States during the Civil War, the common objectives of nationalism did not exist, and at the close of the war boundary lines remained where they had been before the conflict started.

The theory of militarism holds that in every country there is a military caste which thrives on the perpetuation of the heroic traditions of its ancestors. With an increase in the power of the military caste comes increased power and wealth for those who provide supplies for the military organization surrounding this caste. Much has been written to prove the influence of great international syndicates and cartels of munition makers upon such military castes. But in the jungle tribes of Africa, Malaya and South America no military castes were implemented by armament manufacturers. It was the custom for each warrior to make his own bows and arrows. In some of these areas, warfare is still conducted in this primitive and individualistic manner.

The theory of imperialism holds that, as the population and industry within a nation increase and internal forces grow stronger, the nation must expand in order to accommodate its overflowing population and to seek new markets for the products of its industries. The capitalistic system supposedly spawns a proud and militant nationalism, a traditional military caste with a thirst for power, economic pressures, a glorification of war and a frequent desire to spread a national religion. However, the entry of the United States into World War I was "to make the world safe for democracy." Afterwards, at the peace table, other major powers fought greedily for every scrap of territory they could get, while the United States asked for neither annexations nor indemnifications.

So it can be seen that such broad generalizations about the causes of wars are faulty. We must narrow our vision and instill in it a more penetrating quality. We are left with no alternative but to look within each individual at the inborn need for stimulation and conflict in varying degrees. Whether we like the idea or not, we are going to have to give a long, hard, appraising look at those tiny adrenal glands lying on top of the kidneys and assess the power they have over human behavior. We must learn to accept the idea that great influence can be totally unrelated to size in certain instances. War is and has been for some time one of the principal economic stablizers of society. It requires a tremendous stretch of our reasoning faculties to relate such a small part of the human body to war and world economy. Yet the link exists, and it will take the concentration and cooperation of the globe's keenest minds to lead us, step by step, out of the frightening situation in which we find ourselves.

To return to a single thread in the enormous tapestry of modern life, adrenaline production and utilization per man is greater during physical combat on the battlefield than under any other circumstance. Whether the engagement is hand to hand on the ground or among fighter jets in the sky, there is the incomparable exhilaration of the effort to destroy one another. War becomes glorious. Sir Winston Churchill once complained that modern mechanization was robbing war of its glory, so that it was no longer a gentleman's game.

To experience the excitement of warfare, men will abandon their sexual mates, go without food and sleep, risk their lives and ruin their health in tireless pursuit of the dynamic satisfaction to be found only in the stimulation of combat. In seeming contradiction to the above, soldiers in combat for the first time show symptoms of apprehension and fright. They may suffer from a rapidly pounding heart, pain in the chest, breathlessness, heavy sweating, dizziness or fainting spells, headaches, blurred sight and tremors. When they first experience heavy guns, some of them may defecate in their clothes, urinate involuntarily and vomit because of the volume of noise and the concussion from the explosion of heavy shells. Their fearful response carries with it the prospect of imminent death. The emptying of the stomach, bowels and bladder may be nature clearing the decks for action or they may simply be side effects as the body mobilizes itself for conflict.

Seasoned fighters become exhilarated and look forward to fighting. A thrilling experience comes in combat which cannot be duplicated anywhere else, even though a number of severe battles and lost buddies and other mangled dead and wounded may cause a lowering of morale.

Once a soldier becomes accustomed to rifle fire, it seems to lend a heady, exhilarating effect, but the same cannot be said of artillery fire. Such bombardment is found to have a harmful effect on the individual soldier because of his inability to tolerate overstimulation from fear. This is commonly referred to as "battle fatigue," and if the man is not returned to the rear for a rest his future fighting will lack the sustaining determination and vitality it needs. Most emotionally depleted men, given a rest and good food for a few days, become eager and even beg to return for fresh attacks upon the enemy. Since this is true of the mercenary soldier as well as the patriotic one, it is possible to deduce that definite needs for the repetition of bloody conflict exist, even though life is imperiled. The average professional soldier looks forward to combat in much the same way the fireman of the old days eagerly awaited the ringing of the fire gong. The motivation is the same. Fear produced by danger arouses the production of adrenaline, which is pleasantly stimulating.

The greatest ferocity on the battlefield is found in bayonet fighting at such close grips that rifle fire is impossible. Since in most cases one of the contestants must die, their emotions are so aroused that all sense of pity is routed by the urge to survive. Fear and anger are so intensified that ruthlessness takes over and the men are reduced to elemental, primitive animals without mercy. When one man is downed, he may be stabbed repeatedly with the other's bayonet much as an infuriated beast mangles his victim.

Some of the fiercest struggles in recorded history occurred during the Middle Ages, when battle was used as a means of determining the innocence or guilt of one or both of the participants. A plot of ground was selected and a bier was constructed in one corner for the loser. Each fighter, attended by relatives, followers and father confessor, asked for God's help in the coming contest. After the sacrament was administered, each selected his weapon and the battle began, the men fighting to the end with the ferocity of wild beasts.

One such contest is said to have followed the assassination of Charles the Good in 1127. A knight named Guy was challenged for complicity in the crime by another named Herman. Both were renowned warriors. Guy speedily unhorsed Herman and with his lance prevented him from remounting. Then Herman disabled Guy's horse and the combat was renewed on foot with swords as weapons. Equally skilled in using the broadsword, they continued until fatigue compelled them to drop the heavy swords and shields and engage in wrestling. Guy threw Herman, fell upon him and beat him in the face with his gauntlets until he was apparently senseless. But, with great cunning, Herman slipped one hand beneath his opponent's coat of mail and, grasping Guy's testicles, wrenched them away with a mighty effort, causing Guy's immediate death.

As far back as our knowledge goes, war was the prime problem of mankind. It still is. Yet underlying causes have never been completely and clearly defined. History provides an overabundance of evidence about how the strands of warfare are inextricably interwoven with the forces of mass fear, hatred and a conditioned dependence on conflict and emotional stimulation. And in our own time we have seen awesome developments. Our scientific advances have far outstripped our ability to understand one another and to live together in friendship and brotherhood.

World leaders talk about peace while they whet their knives. Billboards and the fronts of buildings in Russia often have on them a single word—PEACE. This is a device for psychologically preparing the populace for war. It is ironic that the word itself arouses thoughts of war. Those antagonistic thoughts are followed by a sense of danger on a national level, with an accompanying fear of and hatred for the adversary and a gradual buildup of dependence on more individual stimulation. The Russians are not alone in having this reaction. In all countries, including our own, great leaders have usually been

war leaders. Glorification and war seem to be almost insepara-
ble companions.

We all have the primitive emotions of fear and hatred
combined with craving for stimulation on one hand and
civilized reasoning on the other. But it is the former which
determines the outbreak of war. Since the mind rejects war as
an instrument of national policy, we must turn to the emotions and understand them if we are to avoid war. Only a recognition of our dependence on conflict and stimulation can
unlock the mystery of fearful hatred and establish the corner-
stone on which we can build a practical program to eliminate
war. Because fear of bodily injury precedes the covert emotion of hatred, a gradual buildup of a subconscious craving
for the stimulation of conflict with great inherent danger
occurs. With an increase in the intensity of the danger comes
a corresponding increase in emotional intensity, leading finally to overt aggression. In order to hate a nation to the extent of going to war with it, it is first necessary that it be
feared!

In war-disposed nations, the level of aggressive impulses of
the people inevitably rises to a point where their craving for
the stimulation of conflict can be satisfied only by engaging
in provocative acts which will lead directly to open warfare.
Similar to the firing of the gun which opens the gate for racing horses, killing of only one individual can trigger the
explosion. A careful consideration of emotional forces will
reveal that the hidden mainsprings of war's origin lie
wholly within the inner nature of man. Thus, in war-minded
people, predominantly fear conditioned as they are, there is
an inevitable sway from fear and hatred toward national
aggression. It can be compared to the fright which stumbling
over something in the dark arouses; it quickly turns to anger
as the person who has stumbled turns and kicks the object
which tripped him.

It might be helpful to summarize the events and emotions
which lead to the outbreak of war between two rival nations:

1. A national awareness of danger is established as the citi-

zens of one nation develop a realization of the possibility of attack by another nation.

2. Attending this awareness of danger is a fear of bodily harm. Fear of such harm promptly subsides if an evaluation of the situation shows no immediate danger, but fear of attack remains.

3. There quickly arises a composite national feeling of suspicion, hostility, hatred and anger, which is a positive response occurring automatically along with the subconscious realization that fear affords no solution to a conflict between nations.

4. Through a national awareness of danger and hatred, the nation begins to take aggressive steps to reacquire its original sense of security.

5. Therefore, the nation arms.

6. The preparation for overt action exhilarates the citizens through thoughts of imaginary conflicts and through adrenaline stimulation. This accelerated stimulation, combined with that resulting from hatred, allays recurring feelings of fear of attack.

7. The arming of the first nation sets up an awareness of the danger of attack in its rival, followed by fear, hatred and the arming of the second nation.

8. Provocative speeches by the leaders excite and exhilarate the citizens of both nations while they build up their combative drives. Exhilaration further dulls the recurring fear of attack.

9. The intoxication of provocative speeches is followed by that of provocative acts because the craving for more intense conflict and greater stimulation is so increased that it can be satisfied only by outward action.

10. With recurring and intensified feelings of fear on the part of citizens of both nations, there inevitably comes an especially provocative incident which brings on an immediate outbreak of hostilities.

This final manifestation of hostility creates sudden fear, quickly followed by a surge of adrenaline and the creation of the state of intense hatred. Brain centers of belligerent citizens become surcharged emotionally until they recognize no fear. Thus the stage is all set for dominance of the primitive fight component of the personality and for the final declaration of war. No emotion-filled potential warrior envisions injury or death on the battlefield at this stage. Fear vanishes when the survival course is inexorably set for aggression. The force of the stepped-up level of conflict and adrenaline dependence relentlessly drives people to seek more danger-filled situations. Like an avalanche thundering down a mountainside, once set in motion such a force cannot be stopped until it dissipates itself.

The study of man's activities reveals that the sum total of most nations' man-hours and money is devoted largely to preparation for war, the engaging in war or the reconstruction required in the aftermath of war. This priority of martial conflict over all else in the life of man points up the universal interest in war. A practical program to prevent future wars would necessarily begin with the recognition of the fact that *released* positive drives compose the basic cause of war. Acceptance of this truth would start us well on the way toward a fruitful search for solutions.

Most investigators have ignored or were unaware of the significance of the physical, mental and nervous changes which occur in people in the emotionally inspired mass hysteria leading to warfare. Others have observed them but have failed to give them their proper place in the structure of war's causes. There has been no suspicion that excessive conflict and adrenaline dependence are at the base of wartime hysteria, nor that an increased consumption of adrenaline raises the level of dependence upon it so much that more and more hostility is necessary for participants to obtain the ever-increasing amount of hormone needed to gain adequate stimulation. Events leading up to and triggering the explosion are usually faithfully chronicled, but the subtle emotional elements which cause the hysteria behind war are ignored.

To eliminate war, we must face the fact that the destructive urge toward it cannot be abated unless man's urge to conflict can be lessened and the overproduction of stimulating adrenal hormones controlled. The universal, subconscious belief that man can deal with war as he would deal with a simple problem in his daily life is fallacious. The idea that he can fight one war to end all wars or one war to keep democracy safe is ridiculous. Each generation is made up of different people. Every war teaches its bitter lessons to those participating in it or to those left widowed or orphaned by it. It is all but meaningless to the next generation.

Instead of basing all our hopes on a single war, we must exercise our wisest judgment and denounce the force of hatred, which is the great by-product of the aggressive positive drive. We must realize that if war were not so fascinating it would have lost momentum of its own accord long ago. Man will have to exert the greatest stoical repression to rid himself of this tenacious vice. In primitive society, there was a need for the powerful urge to conflict and the automatic adrenaline stimulation which occurred in the presence of danger. Through the ages we have retained the urge toward war, but we no longer have the need for it.

It has been argued that war is a population control. With our medical advances, there are less heartbreaking ways to keep the occupants of our globe in proper proportion to food supply and available space. Where religious beliefs do not interfere, conception of human life can be easily and inexpensively prevented. We no longer have to resort to infanticide, as did primitive societies. By the same reasoning, why should we remain slaves to such a cruel and unnecessary institution as war? The human race is a curious blend of paradoxes. It abhors "uncivilized" behavior, yet it tolerates and even encourages the most uncivilized act of all—war!

To stop the people who insist that war controls population once and for all, it must be pointed out that this kind of control is grossly unfair to humanity as a whole. Usually, the pride of a country—its young and strong—are sent to battle. Thus the long-range genetic effect of war is the survival of the weakest, those left safely at home because they are not fit to take their place on the field of battle. Rather than improving the human race, that type of control does it irreparable damage.

The development of "blood games" has even been suggested as a possible control of aggressive tendencies. These would merely be substitutes for war and would undoubtedly take the form of rituals to help people work off their aggressive urges in socially harmless ways. Each year seems to bring the world closer to some of the fantastic ideas advanced in Aldous Huxley's *Brave New World* and George Orwell's *1984*. The very premise that if we do away with war we must come up with something to take its place is frightening. Yet the possibility that it would be only a transitional measure is comforting. The substitute for war would have to be something terribly dramatic, otherwise it would not fulfill the need for conflict that presently exists. Some very real problems, such as air and water pollution, cry out to be solved before it is too late. For most of us, these threats only lurk on our personal horizon. If the creative element of our population could somehow succeed in convincing the public of the extreme and urgent danger these problems present, perhaps the world's peoples could become united against a common enemy whose defeat would truly save humanity.

If we cannot find an acceptable substitute for war, our only hope is to free man from his uncontrollable urge to experience combat for the enjoyable stimulation it brings. If this could be done—and there is hope that it can—all the monetary resources, time and brains now devoted to the invention and manufacture of weapons of destruction could be used to build a better planet. What greater contribution could mankind make to his world?

10

Till Death do us Part

The ancient saying is no heresy:
Hanging and wiving go by destiny.
SHAKESPEARE

ANTHROPOLOGISTS and other students of the history and customs of primitive man state that in early times there was no feeling between the sexes which could be dignified by our modern word "love." In the ancient past, sex was synonymous with love. For example, tracing the origin of the word love reveals that it is derived from a Sanskrit word denoting lust. Long ago, the male of the human species went out and got his woman wherever he could find her and as his lust dictated. It mattered little if he had to kill another man to accomplish his mission. His exciting journey to his cave with his stolen woman was often enlivened by violent fighting, sometimes resulting in a number of cracked skulls. There was no marriage as we know it, so neither was adultery in existence. Incest was of little or no concern, and women were often passed from one victorious male to another. Even within the recent period of recorded history, it was a custom of the conquerors of a city to kill the men and parcel out the women among the victors.

Early Greek poets, with all their revered ideas, showed little recognition of love as an element of marriage. Theogony (the genealogy of the gods) likened marriage to cattle breeding. The Romans of the Republic held much the same view. Greeks and Romans alike regarded propagation as the chief objective of marriage. They regarded any other purpose as wanton and best attained outside of marriage. Except for isolated examples found in some countries, such as Egypt, where women were venerated, the general use for women in ages past was for whatever sexual satisfaction and work could be obtained from them.

The advance of Christian civilization brought about a separation of love and sex, with sex spoken of as something base and ugly. Love was referred to as the divine fire and the two were seldom spoken of in the same breath. The emotion of love incorporating sex as it does in enlightened nations today is a relatively recent phenomenon.

Human behavior has long been known to be influenced by the sexual glands, a fact in sharp contrast to the recent discovery of the close association between adrenal gland secretion and the emotion of repressed hatred. This is because the excitation causing a secretion of the sexual glands is clearly recognizable. Man excites woman and woman excites man. The emotion of hatred has been recognized, too, for a long time, but any understanding of the adrenal glands and the role their hormones play in our daily lives has come about within the past fifty years. When recognition of the action of the adrenaline hormone was added to our understanding of the action of the sex hormone, there was revealed the key to the mystery of hatred and love and to the hidden mainspring of human behavior.

Poets and authors have often expressed curiosity and wonder at the close connection between love and hate. Their writings show that the existence of these contrasting emotions directed toward the same person has long been recognized as a true characteristic of man. We have all observed instances in which love and hate exist in close relationship. A situation of aggression can exist in a home founded on the principles of love. Even in the most harmonious of families, the ugly spectre of hatred is revealed by occasional careless remarks and acts of man or wife. Parents often combine love for their children with instances of distressing abuse.

The cases of rape and assault in our courts give but a small indication of how often sexual passion is closely attended by violence. The physician who is the recipient of many confidences knows how often marital recriminations and scuffles end in happy sexual union. The animal kingdom behaves in much the same manner. Horse breeders know a mare will bite and kick a stallion even when she is in heat and desires him. Observation of the actions of domestic cats at mating time verifies this close connection between the desire to mate and the urge to wage battle. Zoologists, who study the mating habits of larger animals such as tigers and leopards, tell us that sexual congress in the jungle is often preceded by a ferocious struggle. Sometimes these large, battling cats thresh down a bloody circle in the underbrush more than a hundred feet across. These examples serve to illustrate the close relationship between the emotions of love and hate, between the sex hormone and the adrenal hormone and, therefore, between the sex glands and the adrenal glands.

The interrelationship of the endocrine glands, so closely associating love and hate, reveals much about these opposing emotions. The adrenal glands produce adrenaline and when hatred occurs this hormone causes a widespread stimulation of body organs, including the brain, whereas the sex glands produce the sex hormone which promotes the emotional feeling of love. These two glandular mechanisms are located in or near the abdominal area of the human body and release their potent chemicals directly into the blood stream. However, released adrenaline can excite the pituitary gland, which in turn can arouse the sex glands. Conversely, a person sexually aroused without a sexual partner may find his adrenaline in a state of excessive supply as he prepares for a sexual conquest when none is available. Thus the mutual excitation of opposing mechanisms can be a source of frequent alterations of the emotions of love and hate.

When love is dominant, there is a preponderance of the chemical sex hormone in the bloodstream. When hatred is dominant, there is a preponderance of the chemical hormone adrenaline in the bloodstream. In primitive society, where emotions were freely expressed, the sexual act was an attack by a positive male upon a negative female. Adrenaline was excessive in the bloodstream during most of the attack. For a short period, the sexual hormone was predominant, but was quickly dissipated, returning the adrenal hormone to dominance and bringing a return of the emotion of hate. This alternating cycle in the bloodstream of an excess of one hormone and then the other is significant in explaining the alternation of the feelings of love and hate which anyone can experience.

The capacity for loving and hating someone at the same time (ambivalence) is usually controlled and concealed. In fact, a person feeling hatred ordinarily hides this unbecoming attitude and puts on an aura of respectability and good breeding. On the other hand, a girl deeply in love may pretend dislike for the object of her affections. Thus, from a physiological standpoint, distinction must be made between true emotions and mental attempts at camouflage.

Because love and hate are two powerful antithetical emotions associated with separate hormonal mechanisms, their existence in a person follows a physiological pattern of alternation. The changing dominance of these hormones is in tune with nature's plan: the action of one hormone is directed toward the propagation of a new generation while the action of the other hormone is directed toward protecting the present generation from damage and death. Thus the interacting chemicals are concerned with the survival of the individual. Their polarity keeps these two emotions clear-cut, vivid and vital, a common phenomenon in nature. The moon is full and then in eclipse. The alternating current of electricity is first positive, then negative. Day alternates with night, year in and year out.

Not only is there a noticeable alternation between love and hate, but there is also a common alternation between fear and hatred within individuals. In daily situations of danger and conflict, fear is the first automatic survival response. However, in modern life, with its multitude of indefinite dangers, fear resolves nothing, so the positive drive is called to give aid. But angry, outward fighting "just isn't done" among people who pride themselves on their behavior, so they inhibit this emotion and repress it until it becomes hatred, which also resolves nothing. Since the conflictive situation is left unresolved, the frustrated individual subconsciously allows first one drive and then the other to come to his aid, thereby becoming surcharged with alternating emotions of fear and hatred. The same mechanisms operate in married life.

Marriage fails when husband and wife allow their urge for conflict and stimulation to become more pressing than their desire for love and contentment. Often this happens in such a slow, insidious manner that the transition is hardly realized. A quarrel may start in a mild and simple way. Soon the participants begin to derive a pleasurable stimulation from the quarrel and from the reconciliation that usually follows. They find it fun to "kiss and make up." This excitement adds interest to the placid monotony of their married life. In time, their mounting desire for greater excitement makes these quarrels more frequent, more bitter and more hateful, until ultimately a state of adrenaline preponderance is permanently established in their bloodstreams. If they give vent to their desire to gratify this craving for greater conflict and intense adrenaline stimulation, before long they won't be able to remember when they last felt real tenderness for each other. Some fortunate couples suddenly realize the peril to their marriage and exclaim, "What is happening to us? We love each other, but we continually quarrel and hurt each other." They share the blame and pledge a lasting love. Often a new life is conceived at the time of loving reconciliation, marital love and sexual desire naturally being associated with each other.

In other couples, conflict so intensifies that the old love changes into a stage of active rage, occasionally leading to murder. Other couples profess a deep desire to make their marriage work, but seem unable to control their constant bickering. Even with the realization that they are adding fuel to the fire, as it were, they will go on saying aggravating things.

"You aren't the person I married," one may say and perhaps add, "Love is certainly blind." The words, once out, cannot be recalled and leave their mark on the hapless marriage.

The truth is that in most cases one or both fail to bear and forbear. When married partners prefer aggression to peace, the very "milk of human kindness" is washed away by a flood of pleasurable, but selfish and hurtful, stimulation.

Another contributing factor in the change from love to hate between the sexes is the decided change taking place in the emotional attitude of women, briefly discussed earlier. Western nations particularly are witnessing a rapidly decreasing fear-conditioning in women throughout the entire social structure. This basic change, which is altering the conflictive relationship between the sexes in a profound and startling way, gained momentum after World War I. It is continuing to affect all phases of modern civilization, making women more free in expressing their inner urges. How far this dynamic process will go and what its implications are, only the future will reveal.

In the past, women have always been more fear conditioned than men because they were dependent upon men for food, clothing and protection. Hence men gained in stature and emotional power. Some of them, since they did not have to repress their positive drive, physically beat their weaker, dependent wives and derived pleasant stimulation from the act.

Almost everything concerning sex has acted to condition women to know fear. Biologically, women have negative bodies in the sense that they receive men's positive sexual advances and secretions. By its nature, the sexual act is conflict. Women used to be repeatedly and brutally attacked, much like the aggressive sexual attacks characteristic of the animal world. Such attacks are not entirely unknown today. In Asia and Africa, the female is frequently subjected to indignities which members of our Western world find revolting. Even in the West, some brides flee from their husbands during the honeymoon or soon afterward because of uninhibited sexual attacks.

If brutality exists in our culture and lends to marital separation, the true cause is rarely told. "Physical cruelty" has a degrading sound, while "mental cruelty" comes nearer to being acceptable, even though it is often further from the truth.

In the past, women were unable or did not dare to try to overthrow the inherent power men held over them. They submitted to sexual attack, the induction of pregnancy, physical abuse and cursing. Living in this kind of jeopardy quickened their sense of the danger of attack, increased their fear-conditioning and, paradoxically, drove them into their husbands' arms for safety and protection because there was no place else to go. They might feel violent, inner hatred, but they bore it silently, quietly nursed their physical and mental wounds and often retreated into the recesses of their own minds in order to relieve their repressed, antagonistic emotions.

Modern woman is changing all that. In democratic countries, she is becoming decreasingly fear conditioned, resulting in the emergence of the primitive urge to fight which once belonged only to the male. The situation has not yet reached the point at which the woman, generally speaking, prefers to face the world and its accumulation of hatred alone. She still desires and values protection and seeks through marriage the stable presence and the pleasing reassurance of man. She wants a mate and a protective companion. Social custom and law have come to protect her from hostile masculine treatment. Indeed, she is now so liberated that she feels free to express her own likes and dislikes on an equal footing with all men.

In many ways, this increased freedom is a boon to women. The alarming thing about it is that now angry words and deeds come from both members of a marriage, raising the level of conflict and adrenaline dependence to a frightening point. The greater expression of hate provides a background for more frequent drifting from love toward hate. Even though hate may have existed as much in bygone days, families stayed together and marriages endured simply because there was no other choice for the wife. Now the wife knows she can go out and get a job to make a living for herself and her children. She also knows that in most cases courts will see that she gets financial help if she needs it. This is a basic reason for the increasing number of divorces and separations.

As a result of all this, men are becoming increasingly fear conditioned and are experiencing a repression of the primitive urge to fight in their personalities. They are no longer "lord and master" in their homes. They have been relegated to the status of a mere partner. Many "family situation" programs on television show the nominal head of the household being outwitted at every turn, even by his young children. How this development will permanently affect families cannot be assessed for some years to come. Sometimes, a certain mode of behavior swings like a pendulum from one extreme to another. Only time will reveal how men will take this "devaluation."

One thing is certain—men and boys are being physically, mentally and emotionally frustrated. Naturally aggressive males are becoming more fear conditioned, making them passive rather than active beings. They hesitate in the face of mental challenges, physical menaces, universal hates and even remembered dangers. Help seems nowhere in sight, as individual man is a tribal or gregarious creature, and all men are in the same fix. There is nobody he can count on for aid, support and encouragement. He finds himself an unwilling cog in the mechanism of a society he did not shape and does not want. He feels trapped and confused. There is nobody left to dominate.

His emotionally aggressive integrity is further seriously affected by a gnawing doubt regarding his ability to "act like a man." His contact with other men disturbs him, as he does not even know what they expect of him. He wants to be part of the tribe and to abide by its social dictates, and yet he feels driven to fulfill his own proclivities. He is pulled two ways and feels with good reason that his security is threatened. These threats and conflicts are ubiquitous and contribute largely to the nervous strain to which he is constantly subjected. The ultimate result of incessant exposure to unfavorable conflictive situations is that most men become incurably frustrated and increasingly fearful as they make ineffectual attempts to face the uncertainties of each new day's activities.

Thus frustrated, they get no real satisfaction from their mundane, routine jobs, nor from the hustle and bustle of their daily lives. They continually look for things to get better, but somehow improvement never seems to come. They may put up a bold front and seem reasonably successful, but they feel an inner weakness because of their inability to meet the increasing emotional demands of life. Even though women do not intend to be this way sometimes, they are quick to note even the slightest crack in the mental armor of men. They can detect male attempts to conceal frustration and fear. This emotional and mental disintegration of male aggressiveness gives them a new self-confidence and increases their ability to compete with men in a world of universal conflict.

Women can now engage in conflict and obtain pleasurable stimulation from it with little danger to themselves. Laws favor women to the extent that many a wife is acquitted of knifing or shooting her husband if she claims self-defense. The masculine sex, unaccustomed to female aggressiveness, is often forced to endure the indignity of aggressive attack from the biologically weaker sex. While he resents and denies his increasing fear-conditioning and the average woman acknowledges with pride her decreasing fear-conditioning, a fundamental change is taking place in the conflictive relationship of the sexes. While masculine dominance is weakening, feminine emergence is increasingly evident socially, occupationally and financially. Its greatest effect is on home life.

New conflict is taking place between the sexes in every imaginable way. The field of combat is littered with broken homes, ungratified love and unsatisfied sex. Some who study the ramifications of social changes say that this power-balance shift in homes is increasing the incidence of juvenile delinquency. Undoubtedly, this change in the status of men and women will continue for an unknown period of time before it stabilizes.

Hatred between the sexes is revealed as criticism, sarcasm, jealousy, spite, vanity and open hostility. If a woman directs these weapons against her husband, it adds to the increasing frustration man is being forced to endure and rasps his already roughened nerves. Such elements are usually behind a husband's desertion of his family or his retreat into alcoholism.

Some authorities contend that a truly satisfactory marriage is a rarity. Some say that tumult in the home is better than a veneer of contentment. Families in the upper middle class work so hard at appearing respectable that they often hate more intensely and inflict more suffering on the members of their own families than those who give vent to their feelings. Disguising hatred is an art that has been mastered by many.

Since we have actually touched the moon with manmade equipment, isn't it about time we touched on another's hearts with honesty? Toward the end of this chapter, we will explore some ways of banishing hidden hate from marriage and family life in general. Some of them will be old, some new. All of them will be worth a try for human beings who would like to prove Alexander Pope a pessimist when he made that reference so long ago to "this long disease, my life." Even the incurable optimists among us who insist that life is a marvelous gift readily admit that it takes great effort and hard work to reap its rich rewards.

Although our divorce rate is growing alarmingly, all of the reasons underlying it are not new or blamable on the increasing aggressiveness of women. Wives have been complaining that other husbands make more money for a long time. They have been humiliating their husbands in the presence of their children, relatives and in-laws. Such women used to be locked in stocks. No one would advocate that treatment now. Once in a while an angry husband beats his wife up, but he ends up being hauled into court.

Nagging and complaining are just as common when directed by husbands toward wives. Until fairly recently, men considered it one of their privileges to criticize, make sarcastic remarks and be stingy if they chose to. The main difference now is that if the wife is young enough to support herself she will not endure such a situation.

One of the most distressing puzzles of our modern social structure is why marriage seems to stimulate mutual aggressiveness between a man and a woman and cause them actually to work at the destruction of their alliance. All too often, a cold war rages almost continuously between the partners when they should be working together toward mutual helpfulness, better personal integration and creativity. Why does the elation of winning a desired mate often endure but briefly?

One certain factor is that marriage has little chance of permanence when either or both members come to regard it merely as an obligation. This feeling of duty gradually becomes depleted, and aggressive feelings of dislike and even hatred filter in to replace the love which blossomed at the beginning of the marital union, which both expected to continue until death.

The fullest expression of love comes with the desire and complete willingness of sexual opposites to live together simply and naturally, free from antagonizing aggression. Such a state promotes the propagation of the species through the physical union of man and woman. But the harmony can be destroyed by hatred and can disrupt nature's plan for propagating a new generation. One of the difficulties is the natural, primitive aggression between the sexes which makes it hard to abandon their separate identities and to merge in order to rear their progeny according to the order of nature.

Love, hate and fear, all primary emotions, have a variety of interrelationships. Love and its manifestations are orientated toward the sex glands; hate and fear with their displays are orientated toward the adrenal glands. The feeling of love is a human urge to respond with affection and friendship in a situation in which no danger is perceived. Because of the apparent lack of danger, trust in another and confidence in one's inner self are the attributes of the "going-toward" emotion of love.

Love's primal goal—propagation of the species—is expressed in the physical manifestation of the sex drive—sexual intercourse. By that means, sexual tension is relieved. Nature purposely provided the human race with hormones whose action tends to attract man and woman to each other physically, for then the sexual act follows and the future of the race is assured.

However, these hormones are short acting by nature's plan. That was especially important in man's primitive past when he was prey at all times to the great beasts who tracked him down relentlessly. In those times, if feelings of tenderness, affection and love had persisted for long periods of time, man would have let down his guard and would have become easy prey for mankillers. The survival of the human race might have been impossible.

Because hatred is a human urge to respond with attack and anger to a conflictive situation whose inherent danger is recognized, trust in another and confidence in oneself are lessened in the presence of this danger. In ancient times, the overtly aggressive emotions of anger, hostility and rage were much more common and more intense than modern hatred, which is the emotional manifestation of the repressed fight component of human personality. Hatred is commonly repressed today because man's unchangeable desire to express his feelings of anger, hostility and rage freely and openly is frustrated by moral and legal inhibitions which preclude almost all effective aggressive action.

So the covert, antagonistic feeling of repressed hate, with its outward expressions of anger, hostility and rage, becomes a "going-against" emotion. It has as its goal the preservation of the individual and the species, so important in the survival of the present generation. Hatred is expressed through anger and attack, which we recognize as the emotional and physical manifestations of the positive drive. Through its expression, emotional tension is relieved.

On the other hand, fear is a human urge to take flight in a conflictive situation when an inherent danger is perceived. Like hatred, fear has as its goal the preservation of the individual and the species. Fear, an unrepressed emotion, is satisfactorily expressed through flight, the physical manifestation of the negative drive.

So we have the three primary emotions—love, hate and fear—as motivators of human behavior. But, of these, fear has primacy for weakness and hate for strength. Either, in a crisis, will dominate love, because fear and hate are the most powerful survival forces in the struggle for existence.

Many men and women are constantly haunted by the fear that their marriage partners may divorce or abandon them. This fear produces a feeling of insecurity and instability and further weakens the marriage bond. It may take only a trivial act or remark to stir up mental and emotional forces which can bring on a rupture of that bond. Statistics show that more human miseries are brought on by broken homes than the average person can comprehend. Half a million divorces are granted yearly in this country. The father is missing in three quarters of a million homes; the mother is gone in one quarter of a million. Although divorce is not encouraged under present-day social customs and laws, the rapid increase in its rate within the past few decades makes it so familiar that unconsciously people are increasingly conditioned to accept it. This does not augur well.

Writers on the subject openly state that one in three or four modern marriages will end in divorce. Yet each bride and groom firmly believe that their new love will be everlasting. Few enter the marriage state with the mental reservation that if it doesn't work out they can get a divorce. Love between a wedded couple is sanctioned by the church and encouraged by society. Actually, the love of man and woman is the most intense expression of life and should therefore not allow hatred and frustration to dissolve the union. In spite of all this, separation or divorce is imminent in many homes.

A basically good man may have to control his emotions all day on his job, then come home and explode all his rancor upon his wife. The loss of a sales opportunity or disappointment at not getting a promotion may be behind his actions, but his wife will not know that and the hurt so inflicted may make her strike back, or wish to.

Wives are often accused of wanting to "keep up with the Joneses" but many times that goal is just as important to the husband. His lack of worldly possessions may be a more bitter pill for him to swallow than for his wife. His lack may be a symbol of failure that hangs before his eyes every waking moment.

The failure of husband and wife to demonstrate affection indicates an indifference or even an undercurrent of repressed dislike, if not hatred, between marriage partners. A woman who spends most of her time at home may be bored and frustrated by humdrum housework and the noise and destructiveness of her children. Often she goes all day long without seeing or talking to another adult. Modern innovations which are supposed to free a woman may at times add to her loneliness, as in the case of a home which had been equipped with all of the latest devices for the ease of living. The woman who lived there had not been used to few conveniences. Her comment was, "Now I won't ever see the iceman or even the garbage collector." Her words make it obvious that this particular incident took place many years ago, but it still points up the isolating effects that many luxuries-turned-necessities have had on women. Now, instead of chatting across the fence while hanging clothes on the line, a woman turns from the washer to the dryer in the loneliness of her own kitchen or cellar.

True, women have radio and television to entertain them when they are not busy. But since the majority of entertainment programs consist mostly of conflict scenes they tend to excite watchers and increase adrenaline secretion in their bloodstreams. Such stimulation causes them to be nervous and irritable, and they may lose all desire to show affection. Their emotions may be vented upon their husbands, simply because they are the first adults to come within firing range.

Unless a man is a slave to conflict and adrenaline stimulation, all he wants when he gets home is a good meal, peace and quiet, a chance to rest and a little appreciation and affection. If his wife is wrought up to an emotional pitch or if she has had a nap and feels entirely rested, she is tired of staying at home. She craves entertainment and shared excitement outside. Under such circumstances, there is little possibility of sexual, emotional or mental understanding between marriage partners.

A normal man can indulge his desire for sexual union day after day. The same is not true of most women. Some women say they desire union no more than three or four days a month. The rest of the time they grant conjugal rights to their husbands to please him if they are of a placid disposition. If a disagreement between husband and wife develops an unpleasant tension, the wife may refuse her husband's love advances, particularly if it is the time of the month when her own sexual desire is the weakest. If such refusal is persisted in, the ' thwarting of the husband's positive drive may cause him to be hatefully disposed. Under these circumstances, if the husband insists upon his rights, a full-blown sexual repulsion can develop, with far-reaching consequences. If a woman persists in denying her husband sexual satisfaction as a means of winning an argument or asserting a position, the time may come when hate displaces love and sexual incompatibility is permanently established.

Sexual maladjustment is one of the most serious causes of divorce today. Because sexual feeling is a primitive emotion which is aroused when the sex glands are excited, it is a drive which is hard to control. The mating urge is so easily aroused that it may occur any time a man and woman are near each other, for they are mutually stimulating. However, if only the sex glands were involved, the marriage problem would be simpler than it is.

One of the chief difficulties in controlling the sex drive is that the sex glands and the adrenal glands as part of the endocrine system are reciprocally excited. Therefore a latent hostile and aggressive drive is always present when the sex drive is aroused. This explains the phenomenon of sexual sadism. The pain inflicted in sadistic attack on a sexual partner produces stimulation similar to that which was obtained by the primitive male when he attacked another man to get his woman and then attacked the woman to force her to give in to his sexual demands. Man's sadistic pattern of attack on woman for sexual gratification is as old as the human race.

As understanding of the interrelation of the sex and adrenal hormones and their action in the system—how they work with and against each other—helps to clear up the frequent difficulties between married partners. A misunderstanding of a sexual partner can cause misery and self-disgust. Frequently, sexual maladjustment results from an uncontrolled positive drive for conflict and adrenaline stimulation on the part of either or both of the married mates. The sex drive, being less urgent, is pushed aside. Many persons look back with regret to the wounds they thoughtlessly inflicted on those they deeply loved. They cannot understand why they acted so savagely any more than the sexual sadist can understand why he wishes to flagellate his sexual partner.

Wives often hurt their husbands with stinging remarks which are irrelevant to the sexual act. A wife often resents the selfishness of her husband in satisfying his desires with no regard for her own needs. If aroused to sexual excitement without being physically satisfied, a wife may blurt out horrid words to hurt her husband in order to discharge the emotion engendered by unsatisfied sexual passion. Some wives who are treated this way become highly nervous and cannot understand why. Undoubtedly, couples are more happily mated when they understand that the sexual relationship of a man and a woman is inherently a conflictive situation and, therefore, that sexual desire tends to arouse aggressive impulses in both of them.

The increasing difficulties of sexual adjustment between married partners, the frequent lack of confidence in marriage and the steadily growing divorce rate make it quite clear that there is something basically wrong with the present state of married life. The entertainment media of radio, television and the movies are offering an endless stream of plays depicting the hostilities and misunderstandings between married couples and the resulting divorces which are now becoming an accepted part of our modern way of life.

The most tragic aspect of divorce is the bewilderment of young children at their shattered sense of security. The unrecognized, fundamental physiological factor behind these broken homes, divorces and unhappy children is a gradually augmented urge in either man or wife to conflict for the adrenaline stimulation which it creates. Since most divorced people do not understand this underlying cause, they rely on such general excuses as incompatibility, gross neglect, mental cruelty or desertion to justify their divorce.

To eliminate sexual maladjustment and promote a mutual confidence in marriage, both parties should understand the physiological relationship of love and hate. The customary reluctance of a couple to discuss the intimate sexual union of married life needs to be overcome. It is often surprising to a conscientious physician to find on questioning sincere and intelligent male patients that most of them do not know definitely whether or not their wives experience the climactic orgasm in the marital act. It is not surprising under such circumstances that so many marriages go on the rocks. It is the husband's obligation to determine the sexual cycle of his wife and then to cooperate with her in satisfying her desires as well as his own.

If everything possible is done to promote mutual feelings of love, the sexual hormones become predominant in the blood. Even in today's busy world, the love passion is sorely needed. Everyone knows what happens when love is suppressed in the world. Hatred reigns supreme in the forms of violence, brutality and destruction. Passion—with its ecstasy, beauty and gaiety—can undo the work of hate and fill men and women with the exhilaration of love.

Someone once said something to the effect that there were too many corns and bunions in the world to let love run smoothly. What was really meant was that the run-of-the-mill world was too aggravating to let love in all its glory exist for more than a brief span of time. There is a great deal of truth in that idea. All families are beset by troubles of one kind or another. It takes a lot of maturity and working together to keep small discords from erupting into large ones. Some of the big problems and tragedies are actually easier on the family structure because they unite the members into one entity. Small things like unbalanced checkbooks and overly attentive relatives are much greater threats to a family.

Some wives are just not good managers. They do not make purchases wisely, even in shopping for groceries. Some of them are misled by showy packaging, others by the promise of quick and easy meals. If such dishes are good in addition to being quick and easy, they are likely to be in the luxury class, not for young families on strict budgets.

Many young men collapse in their offices from heart failure induced by overstimulation because they overwork themselves in an attempt to maintain their homes and families on too grand a scale. A few realize what the strain is doing to their minds and bodies and give up before it is too late. The present tax structure, wherein everyone is forced to pay a large portion of his income to the government, increases the burden on a husband, for he and his family often try to live on an income which exists only on paper. And it is all too easy today to go into debt by buying on an installment plan. When unwise purchases continue, the breadwinner finds his back to the wall before he knows it. Some wives are responsible for that state of affairs and end up having the proceeds of a life insurance policy but no husband and no father for their children. Too high a price to pay for a set of stereo components in a magnificent cabinet or a color television set? Yes, indeed.

A much too frequent cause of marital separation is in-law trouble. There are many ways in which relatives on both sides can cause trouble. The couple can lend money to Uncle George or keep one or the other mother-in-law in the extra bedroom on a more or less permanent basis. The wife's visiting relatives may be accorded every attention while the husband is neglected, or thinks he is. A man resents being treated casually and neglected in his own home while his in-laws are being catered to. It may be slightly unreasonable, but it is one of the facts of life. It makes him feel that his wife doesn't appreciate him.

In-law trouble is particularly hard on a sensitive wife, whose hurt and resentment can become almost unbearable. The father and sisters of the husband may be critical and rude, but it is the husband's mother who is likely to bring the most trouble into his home. She may be convinced that no woman is worthy of her son, even if she is well aware that he is far from admirable in a number of ways. She blames all his shortcomings, even his drinking or his infidelities or other faults, on his wife, whom she openly dislikes. She may declare that he was a fine boy until he married "that woman." Her criticism and interference may become obnoxious, but her son is caught in the middle and may blame his wife for allowing his mother to upset her over small things. A dependent mother-in-law who lives in the home of her son and his wife may not only refuse to do her share of the housework but also continually object to the way the house is run and how the children are reared. This makes life bitter for the wife, who is usually doing the best she can. Many incidents which contribute to in-law trouble are trivial when considered one by one, but they may build up a distressing tension which distorts the trouble into greater magnitude than it deserves.

Another keen-edged knife that cuts marriage ties is jealousy. It has no place within the bounds of marriage. It can be a manifestation of repressed hate which takes over when love fades. As is said in Proverbs, "A sound heart is the life of the body, but jealousy is rottenness of the bones." Most married couples know the evil of jealousy even if they themselves have never been jealous. They have seen other marriages ruined by jealous bitterness and rancor. An innocent but thoughtless flirtation may arouse a spark of hate, leading utterly devoted couples to overt conflict. Jealousy sometimes arises from possessiveness on the part of either partner, or it may be caused by suspicion of infidelity, founded or unfounded.

Provoking jealousy for the purpose of aggravation or to add to one's self-satisfaction exists as a purely selfish act with the inevitable result of a surcharge of adrenaline in the bloodstream of one or both parties. As this hormone repeatedly stimulates their beings, they begin to wonder how they could have believed themselves in love in the first place. Jealousy, hatred and conflict take over as the daily pattern, and tenderness and affection retreat little by little until they are only a memory.

A reason for divorce which may or may not be valid,

depending upon the circumstances, is a working wife. The trends of modern life are changing, and those who believe woman's place is in the home must be sure they know the motives of the woman in question. Sometimes working wives do neglect homes and husbands. In other cases, the couple is working toward a mutually desired goal. If the marriage is established upon mutual love and respect and a sharing of ambitions, it can be a satisfactory arrangement. Even children, if they understand the reasons, often thrive in a home where both parents work. Evening becomes a time to look forward to for coming together and sharing experiences.

Increasing youthful marriages are another reason for both partners working. Most men who marry young have not reached the state of financial security at which they can provide and maintain a home alone, so an employed wife brings dreams closer. A side effect of these young marriages is a lessening of illicit sex relations and illegitimate births. Modern young people feel that their love should not be denied. The coming of an unplanned baby may seem disastrous at first, but couples who love each other find a way to provide for this emergency and share their love with the child. Even young mothers who must go back to work and leave the baby manage to find someone who will provide proper care during working hours. The young but conscientious mother happily takes charge of home and family before leaving for work and upon returning home. Thoughtful husbands can share in the housework just as they share paychecks. Although outside pleasures are few and must be carefully planned, such a couple can be completely happy and can build a good marriage. After reaching the pinnacle of success, some of them look back on those lean years as the best of their lives.

Delinquency is often charged to working mothers, as discussed earlier, but it has been proven that delinquency is the result of many interwoven factors. In the poorest home, if there is a shared love in which parents and children are all sure of their place, the home may be a happy one and may have a better emotional climate than a house full of treasures which are measured in dollars.

A few hard to convince pessimists say that an employed wife keeps the yen for worldly possessions and pleasures high in the family. The real truth is often that the mother keeps working in order to help give the children the advantages a good education can provide. And as a mother works she finds herself keeping abreast of what is going on in the world more than would be the case if she got out of the house only to go to the grocery store or on other uninspired errands. It is a known fact that one cause of infidelity on the part of a husband is the dull companionship of the "homebody" wife who never rises above the humdrum. He may not divorce her because of a sense of loyalty or because he finds her devoted care necessary to his physical comfort; but he may still seek mental and emotional stimulation from more interesting or exciting women. His loving wife may be oblivious to his unfaithfulness or may ignore it because she knows he will not leave her. Or she may continue to live with an unfaithful husband because she thinks she can't support herself or because she doesn't want to try. If divorce comes, it will often be through the wishes of a husband who has completely succumbed to the younger, more up-to-date woman who can keep up with his mental aptitude. In such a case, how much better it would have been had the wife worked and kept herself trim, well informed and inviting!

Another fact that people who find fault with working wives should consider is that the new trend is to retire workers earlier than ever before. This, along with the fact that the average life span is steadily increasing, means that the husband's retirement income will fail to maintain the family at the accustomed level unless they have been able to save a good-sized amount. Lowering one's standard of living is not pleasant. Couples who have to do it look with envy upon other couples who, because the wife has worked the required number of years, enjoy joint retirement incomes which maintain them in comfort. This is a blessing for children and grandchildren, too.

The idea used to exist that children should take care of their parents in their old age. This concept is no longer acceptable either to elderly people or to their children. Young couples have about all they can do providing for themselves and their own children. A dependent parent is regarded as a burden and a cause of dissent. Parents have come to dread having to live this way, and they try to prevent it by saving for the years during which they will not be able to work. A couple who continue working after their children are grown share this comfort that they will never be a burden on their children.

A sobering thought is that if a marriage breaks up in middle age and the wife has never worked it can be disastrous for her. She has no ready-made outside interests and no recent training to help her earn her way. She has nothing but a sense of failure and futility. A challenging job which has been a continuing part of her life can get her through such a tragedy merely by keeping her too busy to brood about it.

"Incompatibility" is a word that has been much misused, but it can be one of the many causes of divorce. As in the many cases of "mental cruelty" it is a catchall for broken marriages; but it occurs mainly when legal unions are entered into without sufficient preparation. Hasty, "love at first sight" marriages often occurred during the major wars our country has been involved in. The departing soldier wanted someone at home yearning for him, filling his dreams and waiting for his return. The girl was usually blinded by the uniform and married the boy without knowing much about him. Many times, on his return, they found they had no common interests.

Hasty marriages take place in peacetime, too, and are usually based on sexual attraction. In unions held together only by sexual ardor, the attraction soon burns out. If there is no shared interest or enthusiasm, no admiration or respect for the abilities of each other and no kindred ambitions, the passion dies. Yet not all such marriages break up. Love for a child may hold the family together indefinitely in a state of armistice.

If a marriage is entered into without a feeling of true love or a desire to share the responsibilities of rearing a family, incompatibility is a common result. For the girl, marriage may provide an escape from an unhappy family situation or from having to earn her own living, or even from the dread of being an old maid. The man may boost his pride by marrying a younger person or a beautiful girl, or he may marry for money. Marriages entered into only for selfish reasons fail more often than not.

Incompatability may still be the true reason when a marriage fails after the two people fall in love and marry with the best intentions in the world. The culprit may be such a wide difference in social background, education, culture, mental level or religious beliefs that they just can't make it work, no matter how they try. Of course, the knowledge that divorce holds little of the disgrace it formerly held makes it easier to give up trying.

Infidelity is a common reason for divorce. It is most often the husband who commits this sin because his temptations are usually more numerous and he has fewer inhibitions. Before women reached their present status, they usually endured such humiliation and tried to conceal their unhappiness, but today both sexes feel unobliged to continue an unhappy marriage.

The most terrible way by which some marriages are ended is by murder or suicide. The murder may be premeditated, deliberately planned, or it may occur spontaneously following unbearable frustration or despairing grief. Even then, it cannot be the first time it was considered. The perpetrator must be filled with aggressive hatred and must be surcharged with adrenaline stimulation. He can be "adrenaline drunk." It takes just as much determination to commit suicide as to kill someone else.

There seems to be no sure cure for the illness of divorce, but preventive measures can greatly lessen its incidence and decrease its acceptability. But even these measures, consisting of proper education and training in morality, can be successful only when they are instilled at an early age. With these principles imbedded in the child's mind and emphasized during adolescence, we can look forward to a time when we will have fewer divorces and less juvenile delinquency. We know when and where these preventive measures should start. We have yet to agree on how to go about it.

Preventing hate and promoting affection in the home is best accomplished when a husband and wife share common interests. Yet all of us know of couples who have widely varying interests and superbly happy marriages. It must be assumed that they work harder at it than most of us or that they have some special gift for appreciating their diversities. In most happy homes, however, interests closely parallel each other and a solid emotional bond is forged between the husband and wife. They depend on each other for comfort and security. An important unifying force is love for their children and a shared interest in their welfare and upbringing. Many emotionally mature couples adopt one or more children if they cannot have a family of their own.

In addition to common interests, consideration for each other is most important to marriage participants. "Pet peeves" should be avoided at all costs. It is easy to slip into the habit of saying little humiliating remarks before a husband or wife. But when one stops to think that he would not dream of saying such things to anyone else, it helps him to shake the habit. Bad manners are bad manners, no matter where they are used. Husbands often fail to recognize that complaints and accusations from their wives are inspired by a need for an emotional outlet of repressed aggressive emotions. Once they recognize that these expressions are motivated by a drive for pleasurable stimulation, they no longer take them at face value. If the origin of unpleasant remarks is understood, they lose their effect. Reciprocal praise is a powerful force in allaying repressed hate between the sexes, for it gives both parties a feeling of having attained success.

A bulky crate waiting to be unpacked in a New York City museum bore the label: "Glass—Handle with Love." Marriage is like that, with one very important difference. Whatever treasure that crate held would be put in a place of security and safety with as little handling as possible. Once in its transparent case, it could be looked at and admired by millions, and yet it would remain relatively safe. It would take an earthquake of tremendous intensity or some other violent upheaval to harm it. But marriage must be "handled with love" *all* the time. It is out in the open, buffeted by all the winds of fortune and misfortune, tormented and prodded by people and things that have no real connection with it. A thousand tiny vexations touch it and leave their mark. Its fate is not up to only the two people who have promised to "love, honor and cherish." A vindictive stranger may set up a chain reaction of unkind words that carry through the day and are brought home by a weary husband to be flung at a wife who may also have had a trying day. A curious combination of events may conspire to cause a quarrel between two people who love each other but are tired enough or worried enough to forget temporarily the "handle with love" admonition. Marriage may be likened to the most fragile glass—exquisite but easily shattered.

That is not to say that marriage cannot survive truth and direct communication. In fact, they may be its only hope. We have for so long been conditioned to repress any unpleasant feeling and to let it fester underneath the surface that we have made of marriage a pressure cooker with the lid so securely fastened that, unless the partners can control the heat of their anger, only a violent explosion can give release. We must provide more safety vents to keep the container from rupturing.

Most couples enter into the most difficult and demanding period of their lives with practically no training for it. Indeed, a good part of what they are led to believe and expect of marriage could well be classified as "antitraining." They think they are entering a blissful state in which there are no "corns or bunions" and in which love will automatically iron out life's problems. Living closely together serves to intensify most troubles. Those who have had only their own to contend with suddenly find they are saddled with a double load. Adjustments have to be made every day. Children, in spite of the joy they bring, add to the burden both financially and emotionally. There is often a terrible letdown when one or both of the marriage partners wonder to themselves, "Is this all there is to life?"

Men can sometimes shift their interests and energies into their jobs and thereby shut out the disappointment they feel. But what is a young, unprepared mother to do when the front door slams and she faces the rest of the day with a pile of soiled diapers and dirty dishes for company? She would not be human if she did not, at least occasionally, think ruefully of the days when she, too, dressed up and went bounding out to mix and exchange ideas with other adults.

Of course, homemaking can be enriching and creative, but for most women the "how" of it must be taught. Even young women who have the advantage of higher education are crammed full of information they will seldom use. Chores are mundane and endless. Is it any wonder that it all goes a little sour once in a while? But it's an old American custom—we like to make everything look gay and attractive, whether it's gifts or families. So the game of pretense begins, and before the young people know it they are well on the way to building prisons for themselves with no way out except knocking down the walls. They won't even be able to get to each other, except superficially. And that includes sex. Sexual intimacy can become only a superficial act without the deep, intense communication of spirit which should accompany it.

Our young people, by means of all their protesting, are telling us that they are sick and tired of sham and pretense. They are incensed because the older generation says one thing and does another. Perhaps this is the healthiest thing that has happened to society for a long time, painful though it may be. Maybe it will make enough of us stop and look at the games we have been playing and do something about them.

The first step in rectifying something is to face the error squarely. We work so hard at hiding reality that we exhaust ourselves. Truth and honesty are noble traits. Why don't we practice them more often? Our feelings are real, even if they are not attractive at times. If we can learn and if we can teach our young to bring feelings out into the open, we will have taken that tremulous first step toward real and lasting maturity, which we all know has little to do with age.

All sorts of barriers are coming down, lines of demarcation between religions, races and political issues. Why not tear the masks from our faces while we are at it? With our many means of communication, our potential for a keen awareness of the world about us and within us has never been so great.

Experimental centers are springing up here and there in our country. Some of them deal with marriage problems. It takes a brave couple to become involved in such an experiment, for most of us have learned to expect a guarantee of success before we invest our time or money in any activity. There is no assurance of anything in such workshops. The participants are handling the most volatile elements of life—human emotions. They are often asked to tell things in front of other couples which they have never even admitted to themselves.

One caution here—such groups must have an experienced, qualified leader. The idea is not to argue but to reveal. Group therapy is no longer a new idea, but this particular phase of it is a daring innovation. Once a courageous person brings a hateful emotion out into the open, it becomes easier for others to do so. The participants find that the emotions they have been so ashamed of are not theirs alone—they are common to most married couples. They learn that hate is as old as time itself and that it is a perfectly normal feeling. They learn that it, along with the whole spectrum of human emotions, is common in marriage. It is not hate itself, but the repression of it, that warps and twists the personality. The proper expression of resentment and hate has a purifying, cleansing action. With proper guidance, revelations of formerly hidden feelings can give a marriage new depths and soaring heights, new values never imagined before.

A bonus that seems to follow for those who find success in such outgoing workshops as described above is that the couples who become better adjusted to each other and to life find time and energy left over to tackle problems outside the home and family.

Of course, preventive measures are far better than the tedious process of undoing damage already done in marriages. The day may not be far off when we will discard the old deceptions and disguises in marriage and meet its challenges head on with the brightst weapon yet—truth!

11

The Myth of the Forty-Hour Week

He hath no leisure who useth it not.
GEORGE HERBERT

PEOPLE the world over must wonder who is the real American—he who lives through the forty-hour week and plays away long weekends or the hard-driving businessman who often dies of illnesses caused by stress before he is old enough to enjoy the fruits of his labors? The answer is not simple. It is true that the cultivation of leisure has become one of our major industries. That in itself is a suspicious state of affairs. We take our recreation seriously. We work at it. Is it, then, still play?

The word "stress" can also get us into trouble. If we define it broadly as the sum total of energy-consuming, tension-building activities to which a person commits himself, then the average American works a lot harder than most people in other countries. Some three and a half million American males hold down two jobs. The rest spend about one third of each weekday at work. But what do they do with the rest of their time that is not spent sleeping?

The pace of modern life is stressful in the extreme. It includes entertaining for business rather than pleasure, worrying about accomplishing something significant in the world, maneuvering for an advantageous position in business where personality is as important as skill, serving on committees and boards because it is a civic duty, working at extra jobs now and then to increase income and engaging in do-it-yourself projects to diminish costs. Working hard at being a good

123

husband and father are also part of the game. So is "active leisure"—doing something worthwhile and positive in one's spare time instead of just relaxing and whiling away the hours. Even getting to and from work is full of stress for many of us. The most intense physical effort and the most exasperating and frustrating experiences of the day often occur at these times. Traffic jams and wasted hours on freeways add their impact to the other strains on our time and frayed nerves. Relaxation and creative thinking are out of the question when alertness to traffic situations is vital to survival.

In short, the forty-hour week is an illusion. American males and many females are under stress much of the time they are not sleeping. And considering the growing consumption of tranquilizers, alcohol and barbiturates, to say nothing of the great interest in how-to-relax books, they seem to be working just as hard at sleeping as at everything else.

Of course, this pattern of work habits and stress does not apply to everyone. Some people loaf, take it easy when they can and avoid effort beyond that which is necessary to make an ordinary living. But they are not typical in America. Activity, not indolence, is the dominant trait of people here.

Does the stressful life apply only to white-collar workers? Do unskilled workers, for example, also feel the same pressures? Apart from economics, it is true that many of the stresses experienced by the American middle class are less evident among laborers. But statistics show that people now employed in the white-collar or middle class category now comprise over half the employed males in our country, and the percentage is rising rapidly. As would be expected, the percentage of farm and industrial laborers has declined. The remainder, which includes farmers, farm managers, operators and service workers, are just as likely to be of the white-collar mind in their work habits and aspirations as is the man who takes home a briefcase.

Thus more and more Americans pattern their lives after the men described in William Whyte's *The Organization Man:*

They are the ones of our middle class who have left home, spiritually as well as physically, to take the vows of the organization life, and it is they who are the mind and soul of our great self-perpetuating institutions. . . . The corporation man is the most conspicuous example, but he is only one, for the collectivization so visible in the corporation has affected almost every field of work. Blood brother to the business trainee off to join du Pont is the seminary student who will end up in the church hierarchy, the doctor headed for the corporate clinic, the physics Ph.D. in the government laboratory, the intellectual on the foundation-sponsored team project, the engineering graduate in the huge drafting room at Lockheed, the young apprentice in a Wall Street law factory. They are all, as they so often put it, in the same boat.

Why is living so stressful in America today? The reasons are complex and the roots go deep. Many Americans, especially males, work as though they were prodded to do things which wouldn't or couldn't be done at another place or time. The reason is probably that the old Puritan tradition that hard work is a virtue and idleness a sin is deeply ingrained in many Americans. There was no place for the idle rich in our colonial and pioneer societies, and this notion has carried over to the present with the result that the richest American men are usually the busiest executives. Respect for wealth and worship of work are intimately connected, so much in fact that there is a disposition to consider that all men, whatever their wealth, should work at something real and visible. Even the man who dreams of making a million dollars and retiring sometimes makes his million only to find that he doesn't really wish to retire. If he does, he feels guilty.

Society acts as a group or team to spur individual members onward to greater performance. There is no letup in the pressure to become a good "mixer" in the community as well as a good provider for the family. As time goes on, more and more American men seem to be doing things they think their neighbors and associates expect them to do—devoting themselves to increasingly routine work in the office, taking business problems home for further study, devoting what energy is left on weekends to community service.

If an American casts off the Puritan tradition, he finds that he is up against the pressure of public opinion. Employers expect their men to be a credit to the firm both on and off duty. Public opinion is a tyrant wearing a benign mask.

America's high standard of living has long been taken for granted, but inflation keeps pace with it. Therefore the American worker must labor longer or harder to continue to buy and consume in a manner consistent with his position. Conspicuous expenditure is the way to show that one has made good. Sometimes this necessitates a constant search for a better position or a working wife. Husbands are expected to be partners in a marriage. With servants rare, many men find themselves doing more hard work at home every evening. Many wives urge their husbands to stop working so hard. Yet few of them would like to lower their standard of living. The American society is matriarchal, and many men feel that they have to keep proving their masculinity over and over again by accomplishing all sorts of things. Is it any wonder that women in America live longer than men?

Anyone who has the blues in America is urged to *do something*. Solitude is a condition the average American is terrified of. So he fills his weekends with social, athletic and community activities. He is often weary at the beginning of a weekend and completely exhausted at the end of one.

Ambition is an admirable trait, but it can be overdone. Our frontiers are gone, with the exception of space, but millions of Americans still go from place to place, driven by a quest for better lives. Being a member of an open-class society, he can move up the ladder of success with no limit to his aspirations. Opportunity is one thing; the compulsion to move upward every moment of one's life is another. A person pays a terrible price in terms of stress each time he moves up another rung. Our high rates of alcoholism, homicide and drug addiction attest to that. But far more widespread and insidious is the effect that stress has upon body organs and their function. Less dramatic disturbances are the greater villains.

Neurasthenia is a condition of debility characterized by feelings of fatigue, worry, inadequacy, lack of zest and interest and often headaches. Almost all parts of the body can be involved. Its sufferers are usually people who are chronically depressed and have few real interests. They have a great deal of repressed hostility and are irritable, anxious and worried, even when things are going well. Sometimes these people will work themselves into a passion to gain reinvigoration, then be gentle and affable until the next urge to conflict hits them.

Such people seek excitement and become conditioned to adrenaline production and consumption. If they are prevented from getting the conflict they desire, they suffer from adrenaline hangover, which is similar to the feeling the alcoholic finds himself experiencing when he cannot get a drink. In addition to that torture, the nervous mechanism may simply wear down from the constant attrition of overstimulation. Nervous tissue simply ceases to function from pure exhaustion.

Nervous indigestion is another ailment caused by stress. Symptoms can change and victims often eliminate one article of food after another from the diet in the hope of finding one offending culprit, an impossible task. It was known as far back as the time of Hippocrates that the emotions affect the stomach and the intestines. Nearly every emotion causes the stomach to react. When fear, anger and repressed hatred are aroused, sympathetic nerve impulses and large quantities of adrenaline released into the circulation act on it to dry up glandular secretions, severely limit blood supply and retard or stop muscular activity except at the outlet of the stomach, which clamps down and closes, compounding troubles by trapping stagnant food inside. Subtle gastric and mental changes take place, but they are revealed only through studies of the physiologist. In this regard, Dr. Walter B. Cannon commented:

The importance of avoiding so far as possible the initial states of worry and anxiety, and of not permitting grief and anger and other violent emotions to prevail unduly, is not commonly understood. . . . Just as feelings of comfort and peace of mind are fundamental to normal digestion, so discomfort and mental discord are fundamental to disturbed digestion.

An adult's nervous stomach has its origin in childhood. Distressing symptoms originating in the stomach are prone to occur when a child is subjected daily to sessions of faultfinding during meals. Since the child has no voluntary control over his stomach, this organ gradually becomes accustomed to responding habitually to the fear aroused by the danger of humiliation at mealtime. This is psychoneurosis of the stomach, a functional disturbance caused by psychic factors alone. From the standpoint of the conditioned reflex, how does this happen? A psychic experience happens coincidentally with a somatic symptom. For example, the smell of food and the gastric secretion stimulated by a meal come at the same time. Later, the same somatic symptom may occur without somatic cause merely in response to the same psychic experience—in this case, the smell of food without a meal. If humiliation and the smell of food are experienced repeatedly at mealtime, gastric secretion will be stopped and the stomach's function will be disturbed. Later, merely the smell of food will produce the unfavorable gastric response without a meal. A conditioned state of chronic nervous indigestion has supervened when food is smelled, without humiliation, and still an upset stomach results.

Symptoms characteristic of digestive tract ulcers are at least as old as Christianity. In A. D. 20 Celsus took notice of the relationship of stress to such symptoms during military compaigns. The relationship of psyche to soma is still controversial nineteen centuries later.

Much experimental work has been done since World War II. Dr. Harold Wolff and his collaborators had an interesting patient, Tom, who had a fistula. Through this "window" it was possible to observe that, in conversations with him which produced mental stress, Tom's stomach lining became reddened and engorged with blood by vascular dilatation and wet with gastric juice of high acidity, thereby rendering it temporarily fragile and subject to ulceration. The investigators even took brilliant color photographs of the process. Tom's earlier life experience had been filled with frustration and disappointment, leading to his becoming fear conditioned. His desire for aggression was repressed, so his stomach malfunctioned in an attempt to restore relative physiological constancy when psychic tension occurred.

A similar patient, observed by others, displayed exactly opposite reactions. The gastric lining blanched and there was a decrease in the secretion of gastric acid. This convinced Harold Wolff more than ever that he was on the right track, because the reaction occurred in a different person under other circumstances. And this patient was less fear conditioned by past experiences.

Patients who have peptic ulcers secrete more gastric juice than normal people and, what is more important, they secrete more when no obvious stimulant is present—throughout the night, for instance. Although these patients are shielded from the sight, odor or taste of food at night, a continuous, excessive secretion is regularly found. The vagus nerves do the stimulating, although just how remains obscure. Tension and strain may pay off in hyperactivity or it may be that the repressed emotions of the waking mind are reactivated during sleep to further stimulate these nerve centers.

Heart disorders have increased more than 400 percent since the beginning of this century. Coronary disease is an affliction characteristic of men in middle age; women become more vulnerable with increasing age. The heart is the focal point of nervous anxiety in fear-conditioned people. Many diseases are more painful than heart attacks, but they do not have the element of overpowering nervous anxiety. Pascal rightly said, "The heart has its logic which reason cannot apprehend."

Great amounts of fatty acids, cholesterol and adrenaline are present in force in the bloodstream during periods of emotional excitement. When emotional outlets are blocked, the result is a state of chronic overstretching of coronary blood vessel walls. The walls are thickened by deposits of cholesterol, which later may form a thrombus, or blood clot.

Great amounts of adrenaline accelerate the heartbeat while increasing its force, dilate blood vessels in the heart, raise the blood pressure and further the clotting of the blood. A combination of these factors may cause a blood clot to be loosened and torn from its wall to move deeper into the heart to block a blood vessel in a vital area, causing a heart attack.

The famous Scottish physician John Hunter, who suffered from coronary artery disease, once said, "My life is in the hands of any rascal who chooses to make me angry." He was right, for he died suddenly during a violent altercation.

All the foregoing demonstrates what a powerful enemy stress can be to the human organism. As usual, it is easier to give advice than to follow it. But sometimes, if the enemy is recognized in time, wisdom triumphs and life can be prolonged or saved by the application of common sense. It is possible to avoid a great deal of stress, even in these times. It seems strange, but an illness may be just what is needed to make a person stop and think in time. A favorite saying among medical men is "If you want to live to a ripe old age, have a chronic illness and take care of it!"

12

Sex, Sleep and the Psychiatrist

A woman is a dish for the gods if the devil dress her not.
Sleep . . . the death of each day's life.
Raze out the written troubles of the brain.

SHAKESPEARE

INTIMACY and violence have too much in common to
be considered completely separate. But in the setting of home
and marriage, sex can help channel and redirect trends
toward violence. Outside of marriage, it is possible to substitute constructive activities—although, admittedly, it is a tall
order. Sex without love, illegitimacy and so many associated
troubles will continue to beset society for a long time to
come. This fact must be faced. However, as the species con-
tinues to improve, even with the frequent backslidings we
must expect, more effective means will be forthcoming to
deal with this major problem. An openness toward sex is one
of the hopeful signs. Aspects of sex are now being discussed
which used to be whispered about. Sexual aberrations will
decrease as the light of knowledge penetrates the darkness
surrounding them.

The people of Sweden have long been known for their lib-
eral attitudes toward sex. They are a long way from proving
anything definite, though, since their suicide rate is extremely
high. All we can do is admit that we are still in the process of
emerging from primitive darkness on this vast subject. Each
one of us can adopt a wholesome view of sex and instill the
same in our offspring. We are faced with a lengthy, laborious
process. Archaic attitudes cannot be swiftly changed.

Curbs on pornography have been lifted in Denmark, and

131

sexual crimes have decreased, but it is far too early to say whether or not the effect will be a lasting one. As prohibition drove drinking underground without getting rid of it, perhaps the censorship of reading matter works the same way. Anything forbidden by law becomes especially desirable to some people, human nature being what it is.

No other deterrent can be as effective as good family training. If children can talk freely to their parents and ask questions and receive truthful answers, any suggestion of lewdness in human sexuality is automatically removed.

The psychologist and the physiologist, each in his own way, have been striving to fill one of the last great gaps in human knowledge—what is unknown about the nature of the mind and its relation to the body in health and in illness. But the manner in which each professional researcher approaches the problem indicates that their ideas are contradictory.

The physiologist seeks a solution to the nature of mental processes in the functioning of the higher regions of the nervous system. He employs experimental methods to uncover facts and laws of reflex and biochemical activity in the brain.

On the other hand, psychologists such as Freud pursue the same objectives within the limits of the mind itself. Freud sought to discover the mechanism of mental processes by probing minds—his own and his patients'. His position was that although mental activity is a function of the brain it is nevertheless an independent phenomenon, and that a scientific psychology and psychiatry can be constructed without the benefit of cerebral physiology. But the physiologist's position with regard to psychology and psychiatry is that they cannot become exact sciences without being based on the physiology of higher nervous activity.

For several decades the tradition behind the physiological approach to mental illness has lain partially dormant under the impact of psychoanalysis. However, in the past few years certain sections of inquiry in American psychiatry have veered from psychoanalysis toward a physiological, biological and chemical approach to mental disturbances. This trend has occurred because of the high and still rising incidence of mental illness in the United States, and because psychoanalysis has not proved to be an effective method of cure. For one thing, it is impossible to have enough analysts to provide individual treatment. Group therapy is within the reach of people of average income, and there is something about discussing deep and pressing problems with others who have similar crises in their lives that helps gregarious man open up more easily than he does in a one-to-one situation. A person is often surprised and reassured to learn that the thoughts he considered so vile and terrible are not unique—that they are, in fact, common. This knowledge frequently causes him to take a fresh look at himself, to make a new assessment of his personality. He may discover that he is nearer to being normal than he thought. This alone is indeed a vital step toward a cure.

Research has led many psychiatrists toward a chemical concept of psychoses. In human volunteers, injections of mescaline or LSD taken by mouth produce alterations in perception and bodily sensations closely resembling schizophrenia. Also noticed in such experiments are changes in the sense of time and one's bodily image, leading to impaired integration and fragmentated mental processes, likewise indicative of schizophrenia if not deliberately brought about under laboratory conditions.

Oxidized, or "pink," adrenaline solution containing adrenochrome when injected into human volunteers produces psychoses similar to those produced by mescaline and LSD. Injections of adrenaline into schizophrenic patients have greatly aggravated their symptoms. Conversely, other drugs have been beneficial in the treatment of mental illness. The discovery of these various drug actions has given new and powerful impetus to the trend toward a scientific orientation in psychiatry.

It was through his study of dreams that Freud determined the mental characteristics of sleep to be primitive narcissism and hallucinatory wish fulfillment. As a regression to primitive narcissism (an intrauterine state), sleep signifies that the person has withdrawn all interest from the external world and concentrated it on himself. But primitive narcissism also implies a sexual love of self—treating oneself as a sexual object. Thus in dreams it is always the dreamer who plays the chief part in each scene. Frequently, the scenes are sexual in nature. As a person's interest in the external world is withdrawn and concentrated on self-love, cathexes of repressed sexual instincts are heightened and threaten to disturb sleep by forcing their way into consciousness, which would in turn awaken the sleeper.

The defense of the mental apparatus against disturbances of sleep from this internal, unconscious pressure is hallucinatory wish fulfillment; that is, unconscious wish impulses are presented in dreams as already fulfilled. Unconscious pressures are thereby released and sleep may continue.

According to Pavlov, human sleep is an inhibition which originates in the highest part of the brain and spreads gradually over the entire cortex and down into lower levels. The center for speech, being the highest part of the cortex, is first to pass at least partially into the inactive state of sleep. Since the fusion of reflexes is organized and regulated by the speech center, any inhibition of that center leaves the two remaining centers (sensory and unconditioned reflex) more or less disorganized and unregulated. Thus, in the brief transition from waking state to full sleep, there is a short period of time during which the two lower centers function without full organization and regulation by the highest.

People dream during this transitional period and during the corresponding transitional period of waking up. According to Pavlov, dreams are the product of some specific dissociation of the three centers of higher nervous activity, which occurs in transitional periods between the onset of sleep and full sleep, and between full sleep and the waking state. This state of dissociation in the cortex lends dreams their vivid sensory images and their chaotic and illogical character. In addition, the liberation of the two lower centers permits the emotional release of their processes, especially those which depend upon experiences of the more or less recent past and particularly of the day before.

Thus Freud determined that dreams allow for the release of unconscious pressures, while Pavlov believed that dreams allow for the release of conditioned and unconditioned processes. Within the scope of the present work, dreams are considered to be a mechanism for partial or complete gratification of conditioned physiological needs—the need to express emotionally and physically a positive, negative or repressed drive through the resolution of conflict and the need for pleasurable stimulation which has not been satisfied in conflicts of the immediate past, especially of the preceding day.

The introverted, nonaggressive individual has dreams whose nature is determined by the repressed negative drive. Such a drive manifests itself emotionally as nervous anxiety and physically as muscular tension, both in the dream and in the real world. Hence, while dreaming, the nonaggressive individual is nervous, anxious and afflicted with muscular twitching as a result of hallucinations in which he is attacked or frustrated. He may be attacked in any of various ways by someone or something overpowering him physically or mentally. Also, he may be frustrated in various ways, finding it impossible to climb to the top of a precipice, being unable to escape from some abhorrent object or being unable to complete a sexual act. However, if repression is stirred with the release of the negative drive, the dreamer finds himself in fearful flight. When he awakes, he may be covered with perspiration, be shaken by laborious breathing and have a rapidly pounding heart as a result of drive release and the adrenaline stimulation of bodily organs and tissues.

On the other hand, dreams of the extroverted, aggressive individual are determined by a positive drive. When released, such a drive is expressed emotionally in the form of anger, rage, hostility, etc., and physically in the form of attack, both in the dream and in the real world. While dreaming, the aggressive individual attacks angrily as a result of an hallucinatory situation in which he is the one who assaults or frustrates others. An individual whose personality is dominated by the repressed positive drive experiences dreams in which his urge to attack others is frustrated. He feels hateful and is afflicted with muscular twitching as a result of his hallucinations. Whatever form these drives take in dreams, positive, negative or repressed, the goal is the same—the consummation of physiological processes which have been blocked from full expression in the immediate past.

Freud believed that neurotic mental processes followed a prescribed course: when an alarming or shameful impulse arises in a person's mind, it is at once opposed by other powerful tendencies, with the result that the impulse is barred from one's consciousness almost as soon as it arises. Its "charge of psychic energy" is not withdrawn, so the new unconscious impulse retains its full force. The psychically charged, unconscious impulse remains to haunt the consciousness and sooner or later finds circuitous ways of discharging some of its energy. These roundabout discharges constitute the symptoms of the neurosis. Freud called this process "repression."

On the other hand, Pavlov viewed neuroses not as determined by instinctive mental processes but as socially determined by conditions, time and place. He considered environment, rather than the innate constitution, to be the decisive factor in neuroses. He regarded mild "ambulatory" neuroses as being caused by buffetings, pressures and conflicts of life in a sharply contradictory society, one in which there was a great gap between inculcated ideals and experienced reality. Under such circumstances, the experiences of life put too great a pressure on the nervous system. Nervous processes were overstrained, and a neurosis resulted.

Here we can consider a neurosis as resulting from a breakdown between the dynamic equilibrium of man and his environment. The balance between fight-conditioning and fear-conditioning, a certain type of which is established during the course of each person's life, is the mechanism of this equilibrium. When an individual routinely encounters conflicts which are intolerable for him, intolerable because they require him to become active and to hold himself back simultaneously, fear-conditioning becomes inordinately strong. Under such circumstances, fearful reactions result in a breakdown of the established balance. Such a breakdown is the functional disorder of neurosis.

While Freud was elaborating his theory of repression in the years following 1896, his immediate concern was to develop a new form of therapy for his neurotic patients. In a person suffering from neuroses, repressed unconscious impulses and thoughts retain their original charge of "psychic energy." Therapy to be effective must withdraw the "psychic charge," or at least provide it with an acceptable manner of release. In order to neutralize the "charge of psychic energy," repressed impulses had first to be uncovered. This process involved a considerable analysis and probing of the psyche. Little dreaming that his new process of introspection would become a household word, Freud called it "psychoanalysis."

Freud urged his patients to probe their own minds, but he found this method to be inadequate when it came to recalling repressed material. Unconscious impulses which had retained their "charges of psychic energy" were very difficult to bring back into consciousness. In rapid succession, Freud found three methods which could break down, or at least circumvent, the resistance of a patient to recall what he had previously forced out of his consciousness. These methods were free association, the interpretation of dreams and transference. Together, they form the basis for modern psychoanalytical technique.

Free association was designed to allow involuntary thought to enter consciousness in an unguarded moment. That is why a patient is instructed to say whatever comes into his mind without eliminating any thought or image as irrelevant or embarrassing. The patient must talk without premeditation or judgment. According to Freud, dreams were supposed to catch consciousness in the relatively unguarded time of sleep and thus allow free passage of symbolic clues to unconscious, repressed material. The value of such clues, of course, depended on the skill of the listener in interpreting them and applying them to the case at hand.

The term "transference" refers to the intense emotional relationship between patient and analyst. It can range from sensual love to embittered defiance and hatred. Freud interpreted this phenomenon as a reenacting by the patient of emotions created in a former situation, the memory of which is repressed. Such transferred emotions also furnish clues to what is being unconsciously held back. Here again, success depends upon correct interpretation.

For the purpose of this work, the method of free association during psychoanalysis is considered to facilitate the recall of incidents which occurred during earlier periods of a patient's life. These incidents reveal environmental factors which have determined the patient's conditioning and, hence, his behavioral pattern. This dredging up of old conflicts, especially those which took place in childhood, subjects them to the close scrutiny of the patient. He is helped to reevaluate their inherent danger from the standpoint of a mature individual rather than that of an immature child, as he was at the time of their happening.

As an adult, the patient usually appraises old dangers as mild and actually insignificant. Since most people are fear conditioned today, this reappraisal has the effect of somewhat alleviating the powerful effect of factors which in childhood set behavior on the course of fearful response even to indifferent stimuli in the environment. During a protracted course of psychoanalysis, therefore, an individual tends to become less fear conditioned and more aggressively minded than he was when he began the treatment.

Psychiatrists have long noted the intense interest patients show in recounting experiences. A patient undergoing psychoanalysis reveals an absorbing interest in his story, in himself and in his physician, especially if he is encouraged by a sympathetic attitude and an understanding of his motives and the inevitability of everything he has done. Under these circumstances the patient tends to be friendly and to show good feeling and devotion to the psychoanalyst. This attachment is known as "positive transference."

However, psychoanalysts find that after a certain period of time the warm personal interest or passionate attachment of the patient often changes into irritation toward the analyst which may grow into dislike mingled with anger and finally into hostility. This disagreeable alteration of the patient-analyst relationship has been termed "negative transference."

Within the scope of the present work, the phenomenon of transference is explained as follows. It is common knowledge that people derive enjoyment from retelling some particular past incident. In their imagination, they relive past excitement, danger and conflict. Some people even embroider memories of the "good old days" to increase their excitation. When people relating past emotion-charged experiences are subjected to the polygraph, or lie detector, they exhibit physical reactions typical of stimulation by sympathetic nerves and adrenaline—fast pulse, high blood pressure, moist palms and increased depth of respiration. The sympathetic nervous system excites the adrenal glands and other tissues under circumstances of imaginary conflict just as though the individual were engaging in real conflict. The physical reactions taking place and the mental reactions not recorded by the polygraph form the physiological basis for the agreeable stimulation experienced during psychoanalysis.

The phenomenon of transference, positive or negative, is dependent upon the conditioned nature of individuals whose automatic response to the environment is fear. Sensing that fear resolves nothing, the individual turns subconsciously to the positive drive. But social pressures demand the repression of overt manifestations of this drive. Hence the patient undergoing psychoanalysis is surcharged with hatred.

At the onset of psychoanalysis, the patient releases hatred as he recalls his experiences. The patient is emotionally attached and sometimes devoted to the psychoanalyst, who is the means by which the patient experiences agreeable feelings of stimulation through mental and physical release. When all emotion-charged experiences dissipate, the patient is unable to obtain further stimulation. Now he must direct his hatred outward, so the psychoanalyst becomes the target.

Psychiatry is beset from within and without by controversy. Laymen must understand that it is a relatively new field and a most complicated one. Methods of treatment vary, and there is little statistical evidence so far to prove the effectiveness of one method over another. Removing one diseased organ of the body, such as the appendix, or giving a powerful antibiotic cannot effect a miraculous cure. The psychiatrist must thread his way back through the maze of the patient's life and judge the applicability of everything laid before him to the present problem. He searches not only for symptoms but also for the hidden reasons for the symptoms, which are often lost even to the patient at the beginning of treatment. The patient cannot be considered the entire problem. Everything in his past which had, or could have had, a bearing on his present condition must be brought into the open and examined.

Many psychiatrists tend to think that people can no longer be put into the categories "mentally ill" and "mentally healthy." The dividing line wavers back and forth and crosses boundaries too often for such strict classification. In other words, it may be possible to measure the degree of mental health prevailing in a patient at any one time. It must be understood that many factors can cause this degree to vacillate, so new assessments may be made at timely intervals. The terms "normal" and "sick" are not absolute. At some time or another in their lives, most people show some signs of mental illness.

The principal conclusions that can be drawn concerning this "infant science" are that, no matter whether the treatment is performed on an individual or a group basis and no matter whether it is of long or short duration, strides ahead are being made and hope is bright for the future. Already, institutions have cut the time of stay dramatically, and many patients who would have been locked up for life a few years ago continue to hold down jobs, raise families and function much as anyone else except for medication or brief return visits to hospitals.

When full recognition is given to the role which adrenaline and its relationship to conflict and danger play in our daily lives, we may find ourselves closer to the solution of more social problems than the most confirmed optimist among us has dared dream!

13

Conditioning, Our Daily Companion

I ... whom the vile blows and buffets of the world
Have so incensed that I am reckless what I do
To spite the world.

SHAKESPEARE

WE do not live in actual contact with the atmosphere which surrounds us. We are separated from it by a layer of dead cells or by a film of mucus or of salt solution. All that is alive within these lifeless surfaces is immersed in the fluids of the body, the blood and lymph, which form an internal environment. It is the object of the vital mechanisms, however varied they may be, to constantly preserve the conditions of life in the internal environment; but states of the external environment and responses of the body to situations there are associated with disturbances of this internal environment.

If we are to continue to be effective, this personal, individual climate which we carry with us must not greatly change. For constancy of internal environment, every change in the outer world and every considerable move in relation to the outer world must be attended by a rectifying process in the body. Two essential agencies in this rectifying process are sympathetic nerve impulses, which are short acting, and the adrenal hormone, adrenaline, which is long acting.

Many bodily responses are reflex actions over which we have no control. For example, if a skin laceration results in blood loss, coagulation of the blood occurs as a conservative agency. Adrenaline secreted in response to the reflex stimulation of pain increases the efficacy of coagulation by speeding up the clotting process.

142

Exposure to cold weather threatens a lowering of the temperature of the internal environment, so adrenaline promptly acts to avert the danger. It constricts blood vessels near the skin, which lessens the exposure of warm blood to the surface. Liberated into the circulation, adrenaline increases the speed of oxidation in the body at a time when extra heat is needed to keep the temperature from falling.

There are many such ways in which the body responds in an automatic manner. Other responses have to be learned, but once thoroughly learned they follow the stimulus so rapidly that they might appear to the untrained eye to be a reflex action. For instance, earlier in this book an experiment with an infant under forty-eight hours of age was described. The infant was shown a white rat close up. No signs of fear could be detected. But newborn infants are afraid of loud noises, so at the same time the rat was held close to the baby a loud noise was made. After this was repeated a number of times, the baby would exhibit fright merely at the sight of the rat, even though the noise did not accompany its appearance. The rat had become a signal of danger, and the infant had undergone its first conditioning.

Grown-ups respond to signals of danger and conflict more often than to real situations. At a bullfight, the sight of the charging bull and the sound of his beating hooves arouse fear in the spectators, but these seen and heard signals bear no direct relation to the actual danger presented by the bull. Such mechanisms are termed "psychic" or "conditioned" phenomena because they are but secondarily concerned with real danger and conflict and because they are learned.

The nervous mechanism for activating conditioned responses is located in the cortex of the brain. Higher nervous processes there have the same function as those of the subcortex: the resolution of conflict. But in contrast to the rather coarse functioning of the subcortex, where conflict stimuli from the environment signify pure danger and responses are clear-cut, taking the form of angry fight or fearful flight, the cerebral hemispheres make the most subtle analysis, refining and specializing, synthesizing impulses into the total function of the organism. This analytical and synthetical work accounts for the vastness and depth of the cerebral hemisphere's capacity to resolve conflict.

In coping with the environment, two essential higher nervous processes are involved: excitation and inhibition. Excitation, which may be likened to positive electricity, is nervous activity which gets things done. It underlies the positive approach to life and allows for the formation of new conditioned capacities as new problems arise from day to day and require resolution. On the other hand, inhibition, which may be likened to negative electricity, is nervous activity which allows for the extinction of conditioned responses when they cease resolving conflicts in a manner beneficial to the organism. Inhibition does not mean simply a lack of susceptibility to stimulation. It is, rather, the formation of a block or resistance to stimulation. It is a transformation of excitation into resistance to it. It is the negation of excitation, not the lack of it.

Complex unconditioned reflexes alone would serve man for adaptation if all environmental features were permanent. But conditions fluctuate constantly. For example, food is not always at hand to be placed in the mouth. It must be located. Dangers threatening to a person's well-being are often not resolved by attack or flight but must somehow be avoided. A sex partner is not always immediately available but must be sought.

To adjust to the changing conditions of life, an adaptive system responsive to changing environmental conditions is necessary. Such a mechanism of temporary connections, one which arises and disappears with the occurrence and disappearance of changing features of the environment, is the conditioned reflex. This mechanism permits man to seek food, resolve dangers and find a mate by guiding him in the most efficacious paths.

The primary requirement for the formation of a temporary,

or conditioned, reflex is the repeated coincidence of an indifferent stimulus (which may be anything in the environment that can be perceived by the senses) with an inborn or unconditioned reflex. Pavlov's classic conditioned reflex experiment consisted in sounding a bell each time food was given to a dog and measuring the number of drops of saliva which flowed through a small tube leading from the dog's salivary gland. Finally, saliva flowed even when the bell was rung without food being given to the dog. The dog was then said to be conditioned to the bell.

Daily, we are subjected to conditioning influences. The doorbell rings—we expect a visitor. The clock strikes noon—we expect lunch. If someone smiles, we are pleased and smile back. Or if someone frowns, we become fearful and shrink. We sit in a restaurant and read the menu. We can neither see nor smell the food, but words like "steak," "pork chops" and "ham" are stimuli for the taste of a particular kind of meat. The conditioned response follows—our mouth waters. Words have thus become signals of reality, real meat in this case. Similarly, most of our behavior is in response to signals of danger, not real danger.

Other glands may be affected in their functioning by conditioned processes. For example, the receipt of a telegram telling of the death of a loved one brings a feeling of great sadness and a flood of tears, although up to that moment the eyes may have reflected only happiness. And one's sex glands may be aroused by the mere thought of a sexual partner.

So it is with the adrenal medulla. If someone merely sets up a mental image of an enemy whom he pretends to destroy with vicious blows, adrenaline pours from his adrenals. And mental anticipation of great physical exercise causes an enormous flow of adrenaline into the bloodstream. These examples indicate that people are conditioned to respond far more readily to superficial, or secondary, manifestations of objects than to the objects themselves.

Since people grow up under different environmental conditions and are therefore subject to various kinds of stimulation, it is plain that they will be conditioned individually. For example, a bullfighter's son may become fight conditioned toward bulls by watching his father perform in the ring. In later life, conditioned inclinations toward dangerous conflict may cause him to become a bullfighter himself. But if fear-conditioning toward bulls results from watching his father, he may seek a life for himself as far from bullfighting as possible.

Fear-conditioning, as an acquired characteristic of the human race, has become more prevalent as civilization has advanced to higher levels. It represents an experience which has existed for great periods of time and upon which each generation has acted constructively in order to preserve it. The concept of acquired characteristics does not mean that the fear-conditioning of one generation will guarantee that the next one will have those particular conditioned reflexes inborn into its behavior. It is something passed on from generation to generation in the form of facilitation, something which has depended upon past conditioned behavior and which is probably the same as adaptation. When the following generation comes into contact with certain environmental conflict stimuli which were experienced by previous generations, there seems to be a more ready state for fear-conditioning to develop in than was present before. It may be said that environmental conflict stimuli have "fixed" a predictable pattern in the biological history of the species.

Fear-conditioning serves a useful purpose in aiding an individual to adjust to changing aspects of his environment. It regulates behavior to meet survival needs in the narrow confines of modern community life. It is the force necessary to the conformist element of our present social structure.

A delicate balance of fear-conditioning is necessary if it is to be successful. If overly developed, it becomes a liability, hampering the positive urge to tackle problems and solve them. It can hold a person of great potential back. If abnormally developed, fearful responses may be attached to indifferent stimuli. For instance, an individual who was fear conditioned as a child by abuse, neglect and frustration may in adulthood be afraid of such seemingly unrelated things as the number thirteen, steep places, small rooms, crowds, strangers or any combination of strange items or situations. And if such a person were to be subjected to an experience of great fearfulness, such as an assault with a deadly weapon, his entire way of life could be greatly changed. All sorts of external agents—a light, a sound, a certain texture, an odor or anything else that could influence a sense organ—may become effective stimuli only because they once had some close association in time with the frightening experience. It is easy to see how crippling such a state could become.

The severely fear-conditioned individual not only fears too much and too often but also has an urge to run each time he is frightened. Because of this, his muscular system is constantly stimulated to alert and to arouse his body to take flight; but flight resolves nothing in our modern community life. All the individual has left is muscular tension, which can only harm him. He loses a precious part of himself—the ability to behave like a man. He becomes habitually withdrawn and inadequate in meeting challenges. He tries to slip through life unnoticed by conforming to society's demands at all costs and by ignoring his own particular needs. The price he pays for the obvious benefits of civilization is undoubtedly too high.

To further illustrate the power of conditioning, the positive conditioned drive must be considered. It is primarily an emotional process the immediate purpose of which is to resolve the inherent danger of a specific conflictive situation by attacking. Naturally, pleasurable stimulation results. When properly handled, the positive conditioned drive can be most beneficial to the human race. Its physical manifestation is attack and its emotional revelation is typically anger. But, since in man the speech-conditioned reflex system dominates, regulates and organizes the higher nervous functions, the positive drive is dominated by the intellect. Conditioned reflexes to words compose the leading regulatory and organizing component of this system.

Examples of a positive drive expressed as emotional, physical attack are commonly found in men of action—boxers, football players, wrestlers, big game hunters and professional soldiers. Even activities as far afield as those engaged in by certain types of criminals fit into this category.

Creative thinkers express their positive drives by attacking problems of the environment intellectually. This group would include novelists, artists, inventors, scientists, musicians and the foremost businessmen. Their drives are expressed in any number of original ways. The late Ernest Hemingway, in addition to being a writer of the greatest stature, was a man of extraordinarily vigorous action.

The average creative writer, however, is urged on by innate needs to gain power, honor and fame. Lacking the physical means of attaining these gratifications, he turns away from reality and transfers all the energy of his positive drive into the fashioning of his desires in a life of fantasy. With the completion of each literary effort, he has the facility to return to reality. He is fortunate that the world of fantasy is approved of by society. Many people look longingly toward it for comfort and consolation, but to those who are not creative writers or artists the rewards of fantasy are scant. Intractable repressions can prevent the enjoyment of all but meager daydreams.

A true creative writer knows how to take the personal attributes of his daydreams and perfect them so that they bring pleasure to others. He can modify them to the extent that their origin in purely aggressive sources is not readily detectable. When conflicts are resolved in imagination and on paper, he can receive pleasurable stimulation so that the effects of repressions are, for a time at least, neutralized and dissipated for him. In doing all this, he opens to others by the process of identification a similar stimulation. He wins the gratitude of readers and, along with it, power, honor and fame.

The daughter of Charles Dickens told of finding her father standing before a mirror, his face distorted with rage, as he acted out the part of a character in his masterpiece, *David Copperfield*. He was in the process of identifying himself intellectually with that character. He was exciting his own production of adrenaline as he lived and resolved in his imagination the conflict he was depicting so graphically. While casting himself into the role of the person who lived in the pages of his book, Dickens' inner being was almost as vividly engaged in emotional conflict as a soldier on the battlefield experiencing hand-to-hand combat. Undoubtedly, he felt pleasure along with rage, because he was successful at becoming for a time the person he was portraying on paper.

A writer tells of a visit with Sinclair Lewis at his home in Fontainebleau as follows:

> An occasional game of tennis was all that would lure 'Red' from his dugout. The rest of the time he was in there creating people who today are familiar even to the Chinese. He didn't merely live with his characters; he *was* each character. He sometimes startled us at luncheon by acting so strangely that I used to wonder if perhaps he wasn't cracking under the strain. Then I suddenly realized that he was still one of his characters he had been all morning, and he had merely forgotten to return to himself.
>
> One afternoon we all went to visit a friend of Red's, a well-known actor. Because of a bad leg, he was stretched out in a wheelchair in the garden. Lewis, wishing to amuse him, approached him as Babbitt. For half an hour, he improvised Babbittries—putting on a one-man show that even an actor would envy. 'Lord it's no effort,' he said. 'It rolls out like thread off a spool. To think the darn fools pay me for what I'd do for nothing.'

Because Sinclair Lewis so completely identified himself intellectually, and especially emotionally, with the characters who lived in his books, thus entering an imaginary world of conflict, we have masterpieces which flowed from a seething, inwardly aggressive personality. He set down not merely ideas but emotional experiences, too, as a legacy for us.

Tolstoy, too, like all great writers of violence, found himself identifying emotionally as an actual participant in the moving battle scenes of *War and Peace.* How else could he depict such stark reality? A stimulating adrenaline flow made it possible for him to actually feel the impact of events as his pen wrote them down. In turn, readers feel a personal participation in the same turbulent events by identifying with the characters.

Milton wrote *Paradise Lost* while blind. Stevenson wrote many stories of gay adventure while ill with tuberculosis. Gauguin gave up wealth and family to paint in loneliness and poverty. Pasteur, partly paralyzed, carried on his ceaseless war against disease. Florence Nightingale organized the hospitals of a nation from her own sick bed. Francis Parkman suffered from such great pain that he could work for only a few minutes at a time, yet he wrote almost a dozen volumes of history. William Wilberforce, pint-sized, sickly and possessing only minimal physical stamina, put up a lifelong fight against the slave trade—and won! Cartoonist Harold Tucker Webster, author of *Life's Darkest Moment,* was threatened with crippling writer's cramp and the looming loss of the use of his income-earning right hand. He continued drawing in spite of increasing paralysis and began to learn to draw with his left hand, never losing hope, courage or his sense of humor. Eventually cartoons drawn with his left hand were as good and as funny as any he had ever drawn with his right hand. Sustained by an insatiable desire for victory and by emotional stimulation, such creative people could not fail. Some of the greatest deeds have been accomplished by people who were no strangers to suffering.

Sometimes the positive drive falters. Human beings lose their lifelong incentives for one reason or another. If they do not regain them, they vegetate or quickly age and die. Or they may be driven to suicide. As in a watch, their mainspring is broken and the movement runs down.

Edgar Guest provided a striking illustration of a narrow escape from such a fate. His homespun poetry was bringing in over $100,000 a year when he retired at 50. In no time, he was flat on his back, calling for doctors, nurses and medicines. Doctors could find nothing wrong with him. He thought himself a very sick man, and he was absolutely right. He was actually dying from lack of emotional stimulation. His wife finally diagnosed his case. She advised him to get out of bed and cheat the undertaker. He was delighted at her insight. He got up and set to work and soon regained his health. He knew better than to retire again.

It can easily be seen that unconditioned responses such as coughing, sneezing, salivating, swallowing and jerking the hand away when the fingers accidentally touch something hot necessarily play an important part in our lives. Life itself at times can depend on them.

Complex unconditioned responses are also vital. Without them, man could not live and the human race would cease to exist. These inborn mechanisms are concerned with sex, food and the aggressive-defensive measures man must take to cope with his environment and the many conflicts to which he is constantly exposed. Because they have been repeatedly called forth over countless centuries, these aggressive emotions have become a permanent feature of our personal environment, an innate part of our pattern of living.

But it is the conditioned responses that provide the refinements and, paradoxically, some of the terrors of civilization. One of the great tasks before us is to learn how to condition those who follow us as occupants of our world so as to extract the greatest amount of constructive good from their lives without going far enough to nudge them into any of the many undesirable states of behavior. Reason alone is not the answer. In fact, pure reasoning would have kept some of the greatest deeds in history from being accomplished. What drove Magellan out onto uncharted seas to confront unimaginable terrors? What drove Clara Barton, the frail little founder of the American Red Cross, to minister for over forty years to the dying and disabled in the midst of flood, hurricane, fire, battle and other disasters? What drove Lindbergh on that first flight across the Atlantic? Not reason. That would have kept them all safely at home. Future conditioning must hold out the promise of victory and intense stimulation, while maintaining the welfare of others. It is a gigantic undertaking, but one which lies within the realm of the possible.

14

Adrenaline Dependence

He that would govern others,
first should be Master of himself.
PHILIP MASSINGER

RESEARCHERS have ascertained certain facts concerning dependence upon drugs. It has been demonstrated only for depressants of the central nervous system and has not been shown to develop in the absence of a concurrent development of tolerance. Explanations of physical dependence based on immunological concepts, the production of antitoxins or allergy have no substantive basis in fact. The best evidence suggests that adaptation to the continued presence of a drug in the central nervous system involves biochemical changes, especially those concerned with energy-release mechanisms. These may be short lived and reversible or permanent and irreversible, depending on the nature and amount of the drug and the duration of exposure.

Adrenaline dependence is essentially a conditioned state characterized by an overindulgence in the stimulating effects of overt conflict. Under such circumstances men are prone to commit violent acts because their urge to conflict becomes uncontrollable. When reflecting upon the horror, tragedy and bloodshed caused in the world by the release of this innate urge to resolve conflict, we come to realize that most other factors affecting man's existence are relatively unimportant by comparison. In the columns of daily newspapers we can find accounts of deaths in speeding cars, holdups, rapes, murders and news or war and conflict in many parts of the world. When it is realized that most of these evils can be traced to conditioning to the stimulating effects of overt conflict, we can understand just how serious the situation really is.

152

Although alcoholism and indulgence in narcotics lead to moral, mental and physical deterioration, these habits affect a relatively small percentage of the population in a serious way. The numbers seem large because the offenders are conspicuous. On the contrary, conflict and violence are prevalent everywhere. Within everyone is the latent possibility of reaching a state of conditioning to indulge in overt conflict. Within everyone are adrenal glands secreting a hormone which is life preserving yet which can spill over disastrously. Because emotions are held back by social disapproval and overcharged by adrenaline stimulation, anyone, at any time, can suddenly explode in violence.

Three basic factors are concerned with the development of dependence upon the stimulating effects of the hormone adrenaline. The first is the functional relationship between biochemical changes caused by adrenaline and the emotions. Emotional tensions through the autonomic nervous system influence body chemistry, and altered body chemistry in turn reacts upon the emotional life. The function serves to unify emotional and organic processes. The second factor is anatomical and is concerned with the fact that the cellular matter of the adrenal medullas is a modified part of the nervous system. It is little wonder that the adrenal system is always connected in its activity with the nervous system. The third factor is physiological: the release of adrenaline during a conditioned reflex depends upon the cortex of the brain and is therefore an important participant in the emotional process.

Just as the miniature secretion of adrenaline in myriad nerve junctions of the nervous system determines the course of impulses, so on a far larger scale does adrenaline, cast into the bloodstream out of adrenal medullas, involve whole systems of organs in a reaction. Since the cerebral cortex is the highest coordinating center, it is obvious that this important nervous regulator must be determinatively connected with the hypothalamus, which influences the chemical tone of metabolic processes most powerfully. This correlation of nervous and hormonal systems takes place in higher parts of the nervous system, and, for this reason, this activity can be regarded as an expression of the unity of the organism, as a phenomenon of the highest organization, which secures the most complex manifestations of life.

Physical and psychic dependence upon adrenaline stimulation develop especially in relation to more violent or criminal behavior. Such dependence results primarily from the repeated exposure of an individual to the influence of overly aggressive conditioning forces. As a result, the individual acquires the necessary psychological or psychiatric makeup which permits him to receive gratification from a chronic, excessive indulgence in uninhibited aggression and the attendant adrenaline stimulation as a substitute for other types of adaptive behavior. In this susceptible individual, the compulsive, habitual, excessive gratification of an urge to experience conflict and adrenaline stimulation leads to the establishment of a psychological reliance on more intense conflict and its stimulating effects. This conditioned state is termed psychic or emotional dependence.

As time goes by, there gradually develops an increased resistance to the stimulating effects of conflict so that an ever-increasing intensity of conflict is required to produce a satisfactory stimulating effect. This state is termed tolerance. More and more intense conflict must be indulged in to produce equivalent effects. Finally, there occurs a physiological, biochemical and possibly morphological adaptation of tissues to the new conditioned state and to the new chemical environment created by repeated indulgence in intense conflictive situations. In this state of physical dependence, engaging in very dangerous conflict and its resultant release of large amounts of adrenaline into the bloodstream are required to permit tissue cells to function normally. Conversely, when an individual is no longer in a position to engage in the level of conflict to which he has become accustomed, a withdrawal syndrome occurs. This is characterized by one or more of the following symptoms: feelings of fatigue, worry and inadequacy, lack of zest and interest, headache, undue sensitivity to light and noise or functional disturbances to digestion and circulation.

"Drug idiosyncrasy" is a term used by medical men to indicate an unusual type of cellular response to a drug. It is manifested as an extraordinary reaction to the drug, quite different from the reaction usually produced. For instance, in individuals who are idiosyncratic to quinine, even small doses produce ringing in the ears. Local anesthetics in certain individuals produce toxic symptoms. Some people cannot even take aspirin. Others have reactions to sulfa drugs or to penicillin. Aminopyrine may produce a serious blood disorder in certain people. Some individuals who should go into profound sleep after hypnotic doses of barbiturates, fail to respond. Morphine sometimes wildly excites a patient. Thus some drugs may cause symptoms which are diametric to those ordinarily observed and expected by the physician.

This idiosyncrasy demonstrates that people do not all respond in the same way to drugs. A drug's effects are determined not only by pharmacological action but also by the conditioned psychogenic response of the individual. This is especially true in the case of drugs that affect the central nervous system. In the case of adrenaline, hyposensitivity to that drug's effects is found in the lethargic, hard-to-anger type of person, while hypersensitivity reveals itself in the overactive, choleric person.

Cellular response to adrenaline is unusual in some persons, causing them to become dependent on it more readily than other individuals. If brain nerves and body tissues are overly sensitive or vulnerable, a conditioned adrenaline-stimulation pattern is set up more readily. The same thing may occur when chemical inhibitors are relatively ineffective in inactivating adrenaline. Because of innate physiological factors, therefore, some people have a tendency to live a life of conflict for the exciting stimulation it brings. We may say they have an idiosyncrasy to adrenaline stimulation.

Another form of idiosyncrasy is known as acquired tolerance, which is a matter of everyday observation. An individual fails to react to ordinary doses of a drug because of his prolonged use of that drug. The most familiar example of this form of tolerance is that acquired from tobacco. The first cigar often induces illness, but if a habit is formed considerable amounts of nicotine may be absorbed without apparent harm. The tissues gradually become accustomed to the presence of small quantities of nicotine and thus fail to react to it. In fact, nicotine becomes a normal constituent of the tissues of that person's body.

Similarly, the tissue cells of the central nervous system can acquire a tolerance for alcohol, morphine or lesser sedatives. The confirmed user functions very well psychically under their influence. In the case of adrenaline, acquired tolerance is revealed in the individual who seeks ever more dangerous conflict as a source of stimulation.

The pleasure principle involved in conflict is a definite danger signal. Just as it takes more highballs to bring on a sense of well-being, certain types of people find they require more and more arguments to keep themselves stimulated. Any kind of stimulant causes an increased consumption to maintain the original pleasurable sensation. The need for adrenaline stimulation can become as desperate as that for alcohol or drugs. The need to do something to correct this little-known danger is just as desperate!

15

Glands Gone Awry

The deepest thing in our nature is . . .
this dumb region of the heart in which
we dwell alone with our willingnesses
and unwillingnesses, our faiths and fears.
WILLIAM JAMES

MAN, who was once wild, free and prowling, has been expected to turn backward against himself. Cruelty, enmity, delight in persecution, destruction—all these innate manifestations of the urge to conflict—have been converted into hatred and directed against their perpetrators. By this violent breaking from his animal past, man has inflicted on himself a most grave and sinister illness from which he has not yet recovered. He has declared war against his primitive urge to conflict, which was at one time the wellspring of his joy, power and formidableness.

With increasing momentum, man has literally been punishing himself for what he has not dared to do openly since he began to call himself "civilized." He has demanded self-denial and bowed to a social order which insists upon monogamy, and to group will in establishing a system of policing, judging and governing—all in the name of a better way of life. He has nurtured this code of morality in a subconscious attempt to force himself to suffer and to find through inwardly directed aggression the drive release and stimulation he no longer dares obtain through aggression which is directed outwardly.

It is hard to assess our gain when we realize that internal dangers have merely replaced external dangers. Hatred is directed inwardly against the self because of conditioning. Some people are so intensely fear conditioned that they dare not attack anyone but themselves. The danger of possible retaliation from others is too great for them to bear. Consequently, they become increasingly self-critical and self-conscious. They suffer from feelings of inferiority and find they cannot think or act in a reasonable way. Such people have no ability in handling others. They become, instead, objects of other people's wrath because their nervous anxiety is all too obvious.

Sometimes self-destructive impulses are manifested in the need to be ill or in a need to suffer in some other way. Indeed, in some cases the urge for self-preservation is so far reversed by the overpowering effect of repressed, inwardly directed drives that such an individual may attempt suicide. As the ultimate expression of self-directed aggression, suicide resolves the dilemma of hate by giving full expression to a repressed positive drive.

Hysteria occurs in a highly fear-conditioned person whose negative and positive drives are frustrated by social pressures. In an attempt to activate his negative behavioral drive in response to danger, the hysterical person makes an imaginary flight into the recesses of his mind. But this flight does not remove him from sources of danger, so he is afflicted with an oppressive nervous anxiety. In short, his negative drive has failed to resolve danger in the environment. He then turns to the positive drive but finds that in it, too, all doors are closed by frustrations set up by modern social structures. So he attempts to live a life of conflict in his imagination. He practices autosuggestion as he strives to give emotional release to himself through self-directed hatred. Just as an actor gets satisfaction from the playacting conflict of a script, the hysterical person gains drive release and stimulation in creating and acting out an imaginary world of conflict of his own. And just as the actor enjoys the attention of his audience, so does the hysterical person get satisfaction from observing the effects which his alarming exhibition has upon others.

Usually, the early years of childhood show the fight personality of primitive times. But as a child grows older the dictates of modern civilization and the retaliation of organized forces lead to a calling-up of fearful responses. The resulting fear-conditioning then dominates behavior.

What we like to call the "sensible" part of our personality gradually emerges and most of us try somehow to wall off our strong desires for stimulation. Many of us never again become acutely aware of our urge to commit violence except insofar as it creeps in disguised form into our dreams or fantasies when our defenses are down. Even when we suffer from hate and muscular tension, we often do not know the true source of our trouble.

We look down upon the rituals of sacrifice practiced long ago. Yet, in essence, as each individual joins the community as an adult, he repeats the sacrifice of his innate pleasures for the common good. But the social structure is insecure because in each individual who takes up his part in the work of civilization there is the danger of rebellion.

In order to survive under the circumstances of modern civilized living patterns, therefore, it is necessary to accept interminable frustration. Finally, a state of great fear-conditioning supervenes, resulting in a blocking of the urge to resolve conflict by attack. As desires for positive action fade, behavior is more and more dominated by a repressed or modified positive drive. Replacing the gratification attending the release of positive urges are hate and muscular tensions, the former being the emotional manifestation of the repressed positive drive and the latter its physical manifestation.

But let us face the issue squarely. We have passed the point of no return. Even if it were possible for us to go back to our primitive way of life, hardly a single one of us would choose it. We like our luxuries too much, even tainted as they are with the poison of repression.

Our only alternative is to find other ways of expressing our aggressions. One acceptable way in which large groups can get rid of such feelings is by participating in or being spectators of sports events. Let us look at a crucial football game for what it really is. In preparation for the contest, the players and their supporters, aware of the grave threat of defeat, feel a primitive fear of and hate for their rivals. An intense emotional surge permeates the team, coaching staff and supporters so that each individual's production and utilization of adrenaline for stimulation is increased to a very high level, while the intensity of hatred is often only poorly concealed by what is termed "good sportsmanship."

Good sportsmanship is emphasized to the young as a fine and noble gesture. It most certainly is that. But when adults analyze the term it becomes evident that it defeats the essence of athletic rivalry, which by its very nature is open conflict. We are asking the impossible. We are asking team members to be good to their opponents and to engage in serious conflict with them at the same time. The intense emotional feelings of hate and aggression necessary to produce the extra "push" often needed to win a game cannot be immediately swallowed and so destroyed. They can be covered up, but that is only a superficial gesture and possibly far more harmful than an open expression of feelings.

For weeks preceding a crucial intercollegiate football game, the potential spectators identify themselves with the members of the team, so that each feels a part of the preliminary activities. By game time, they are so emotionally drenched they feel as if they were really participants. Pep meetings egg them on until they are bursting with pent-up emotion.

When the day of the big game arrives, the primitive emotions of fear and hate inspire the crowd to cheer, yell, sing and wave pennants. As fear of defeat reaches a peak, a rising wave of hostility toward the opponent blots out all other feelings because of group determination that they must be beaten; thus the emotional outpouring dulls all sense of pity and exhilarates the minds of players and spectators alike.

When the game is over, there is an immediate letdown or emotional hangover for the vanquished. The victors, however, prolong their exhilaration by a wild celebration until they, too, are deflated. Some players have told their physicians that the depressing aftermath of a great sporting event forces them to lie in bed for a day or two afterward. Overstimulation results finally in a depressed functional activity throughout the body for both the victors and the defeated.

Rage must and will find some socially acceptable outlet in group form. The forms society tolerates will differ from time to time, but history usually proves that most of them are looked back upon with a sense of shame. We say we cannot understand the sadistic orgies of mobs in the persecution of the Salem "witches." Yet in our own time we have witnessed the lynching of Negroes, the exploitation of child labor, governmental injustices to the American Indians, the actions of the Ku Klux Klan, the hounding of Japanese-Americans and the savage slaughtering of millions of Jews. Who are we to judge which is the greater evil?

Extreme seeking out of danger on an individual basis is seldom accorded the approval of society unless it is something like conquering a formidable peak against great odds or driving a racing car faster than anyone else. Such foolish things as playing "Russian roulette" make no sense at all. Yet we often read of someone, usually a young person, who plays and loses. The falling of the hammer on the one loaded chamber means instant death. The supreme desire of man is to live. How can these things be explained?

The only assumption left to us is that adrenaline can become as thoroughly poisonous as alcohol, driving human beings to actions that go completely against reason. If enough thinking people care, perhaps conditioning processes may be effectively changed over a period of time so that our young people can grow up relatively free from the devastating urges and reactions to them which have plagued society since it first embraced civilization.

16

What Can Be Done?

No question hath but a single answer.
ANONYMOUS

UNLIKE many species of prehistoric animals who lived centuries ago and perished, primitive man survived the constant dangers surrounding him primarily because of a more highly developed brain with a more effective aggressive drive. A keen mind and an automatic mechanism which poured a chemical directly into the bloodstream gave him the extra power necessary to withstand enemies that unceasingly threatened his existence. By making his survival possible, this substance—adrenaline—indirectly caused him to evolve to a higher, more civilized plane.

Is it possible that the chemical which saved the species is intended by nature to become its master? Or will man harness its tremendous power for the purpose of enjoying more meaningful living? If the former is the case, Darwin's theory of evolution has no choice but to reverse itself to the point where stimuli can be dealt with swiftly and decisively in open violence.

We are left with only the latter choice. Of all the problems that have been brought about by civilization, none is more vital than how to accomplish this Herculean task. Now that evidence is piling up about why some people act and react to situations as they do, perhaps something can be done to halt the stalking of war, arson, pillage, murder and intense unhappiness across the nations of our world.

An encouraging sign is that most people truly want the welfare and progress of mankind assured. Even as they fight individual battles with urges to commit violence, they see that the common good must remain uppermost in their intent.

Sublimating aggressiveness is one of the many answers which hold out hope to the searchers. This process has led man into an exploration of the unknown, to great inventions, to probing the secrets of science and to medical research, resulting in prolonged life expectancy and the control of many diseases. It has led to the control of water for the irrigation and fertilization of barren lands. It has shown man how to design and erect vast and beautiful buildings. He has conquered the air and the sea; he is working on space.

Sublimating aggression is another way of saying that mankind channels his violent feelings into activities which make a better life for all. He "works off steam" without harming other living things. He avoids emotional pitfalls, often without fully realizing what he is doing. He knows only that the world can stand a lot of improvement and he sets about doing his part with any talent he may possess and without analyzing his motives.

Such a man learns to share his products and skills with others less fortunate than himself. He seeks to share religious and ethical ideas with those who are less enlightened. Singly or in groups, he establishes great foundations to further education and research to benefit all mankind. He looks for ways to relieve population pressures, which have built up to explosive force in our cities. He searches for ways in which to further communication among races, so long and so sorely needed.

As a specific example, racial misunderstandings have been magnified and distorted by fear-conditioning. A riot erupts in a city; frightened men in suburbs miles from the trouble go out and buy guns and shells. These men are not threatened in any way, nor are their families. It is just that fright is so contagious and that most of us are so susceptible to it. One misconception is that embittered Negroes and militant young white people are especially strong. The real truth is that the adult male population, which is supposed to govern society, is weak. If we can bolster and strengthen reasonable adults of all colors and beliefs, we will have taken a huge step toward the control of a situation which will only become worse without prompt constructive action. The time for recriminations is past. The time for building a new social structure with a place for each of us is now!

The key words for our grandfathers were "work," "thrift" and "will." For us today, they are "flexibility," "adjustment" and "warmth." Human warmth may well prove to be the saving grace in the long struggle ahead of us. A kind act or word costs nothing, but it may bridge a gap in understanding that could not be crossed in any other way.

We must exercise control over our emotions. If we feel the urge to commit a violent act, let us swing a golf club or build something instead. Let us try, while we are striving to understand and cope with the vital issues surrounding us, to understand ourselves a little better. If we slide back, let us resolve to set a new goal and push onward toward it.

We must learn to adjust and adapt to changing ideas. Lack of change implies stagnation, and that state is deadly for the human organism. There is much wisdom in the old prayer, "God grant me the serenity to accept things I cannot change, courage to change things that I can, and wisdom to know the difference." If we do not recognize or accept the fact that some circumstances cannot be altered, or if we do not realize the existence of unattainable goals, we cannot overcome frustration. Acceptance helps to avoid any misdirection of the positive drive. We know we can work successfully toward changing jobs, types of food and clothing, living conditions, environment to some extent and many other conditions for ourselves and others.

As a start for the completely fear-conditioned, frustrated human being, it is a good practice to set aside a few moments each day in a quiet place just to savor life and the joy of breathing. Such an opportunity is available to the poorest and most crowded of us. Thinking of just one thing to be thankful for is helpful. Others will suggest themselves. I am not suggesting adopting a Pollyanna attitude—merely a few seconds each day to realize that we are *living* life, not hurtling through the world on a terrifying treadmill.

The person who does not let himself run out of goals is bound to keep growing, and because of his fresh attitude he will probably become interested in something or somebody other than himself. Such a person is not likely to find himself addicted to adrenaline stimulation.

Social goals, too, have a way of appearing to be at a great distance. But look behind us—see how far we have come. Many injustices our parents accepted no longer exist. Perhaps, in our time, the goals will come within reach. At least let us resolve to work together and not slacken our pace until that day arrives!